WITHIN THE FIRE,
I Found My Voice

A Memoir

Ruth Redmond

Preface

Everyone has a story to reveal: To fulfill their inner peace:
A journey to conquer and a quest to reach.

When it storms, the geological effect produces a reflection of wavelength or prisms. In other words, it is that rainbow that we all look for with its multi-colors.

During my journey, I discovered the prism of my rainbow that has shadowed me in perpetuating my voice to be heard.

I am thankful for my colorful rainbow: my prismatic coterie of family, friends, coworkers, and even strangers (the breast cancer support group that I am a member and team leader) that I met along the way who believe in my strength and courage. They believe in my testament to my salvation, which needs to be exposed. Especially since I had so much positive feedback from people wanting to hear my story. *Kudos* to my mentors that allowed me to expose my platform to shower my voice to release, soar, and execute my vision.

I have been told on several occasions that my story is relatable to so many personal adversities. I heard their voices, but not my own. So many have poured out their true personal connection. Therefore, I stopped, sat still, and recognized my offering, compelled to tell my story. Below are a few positive affirmations:

1). "Hey, Ruth, I thought about you all night. You have been through a lot for the last few years—a separation, becoming a grandmother, a college-bound child and, later, a divorce. You have exhibited nothing but strength through it all. I have sheer admiration for you and the utmost respect. I'm not making light of what you are going through, but what I do know you have what it takes to get through this as well with this diagnosis of breast cancer. I often ask God why bad things happen to good people. I still do not know the answer, but I guess He has a plan. When someone tells you bad news, there are no words to really comfort them. But I will say that you are a true friend and I love you. You will get through this, too."

2). "Getting ready to present The Privilege of Leadership at the Southeastern Fire Chiefs. Today, I am dedicating this one to a special friend of mine from the DCFD who is going through a tough time and needs all the support she can muster. Always appreciate your friends in your life!"

3) "Thank you. Sometimes we don't realize how much our words mean or if people are really listening. Just know you really helped save my life by being yourself. That needs to be in a book. That type of struggle on top of health issues people can relate to."

4) "Your story of bravery and transparency should be published and put in gift shops for breast cancer survivors."

Thank you all for instilling positive energy in my head and my heart that I NEVER LOST MY VOICE when I thought I did.

I dedicate this testimonial to my baby sister, Martina Veronica, aka Tina. Continue to glitter in heaven that has granted you perpetual light to shine upon, for one day, we shall glisten together again.

I also dedicate this to those who need this affirmation.

Well, are you ready for my story that is filled with laughter, good and sad times that represent me and my real-life events? Then let's venture into my journey of how I discovered my voice to help you find your voice, so hold on and let's go to Chapter 1.

CHAPTER 1

The Family Tree

My parents were born and raised in Washington, DC, even though I have been told that sometimes I have a southern dialect. Back in the day, as they say, families had that strong committed bond. With five children or more (not as many in present-day society), aunts, grandmothers, and sometimes cousins all lived in the same household, helping each other out without the drama (or they hid the drama well). When you got scolded by one adult, the other adults were standing in line for you, too. My mother grew up in a Catholic environment with ten siblings. She was the eldest of the three girls and the rest were, of course, my uncles. They were talented and musically inclined between dancing, tap dancing, singing, and playing the piano, where I inherited the talent.

My maternal grandmother, from what I remember about my namesake, loved her fashion: Garfinkel's, Woodward & Lothrop, Lansburgh's, and Hecht's. She wore her fur and finest clothes. Then there were evenings of her Pokeno games, company, and good food.

My maternal granddad loved his good-smelling cigars and driving big, long automobiles, considering he was kind of short, such as his Lincoln Continental. Because my parents did not drive nor owned a vehicle, granddad was the sole transportation for all of us. Whether it was going to the mall, grocery store, school, or doctors' appointments, he was our chauffeur. However, my fondest memory of him was his singing and tap dancing for the senior talent shows at school and at home. My siblings and I were ecstatic when he used to give us items he found after cleaning up movie theaters after each show. Those evenings of placing my feet on top of his feet while we danced were immeasurable.

Mom's siblings were talented as well. Her brothers played the piano and could hold a tune. One uncle's voice reminds me of the male group, The Chi-lites in which I think he really thought he was part of that group. Other uncles played the piano by ear. Man, oh man, one uncle could listen to a song for one or two days, and Walla, he was playing it on one of his numerous conglomerate sets of keyboards.

The main keyboard had various tone buttons and keys that could play any instrument—from violins to horns, etc.

My aunts enjoyed dancing and listening to R&B songs. My middle aunt, who had a sense of humor and her outfits matched from head to toe, had given my siblings their nicknames, which some folks still call us by them. My mom's youngest sister enjoyed cooking as well. Her golden, fried chicken was the best.

My paternal grandparents hosted family get-togethers and parties. I remember the cousins gathered at their house as we ate sandwiches and drank Kool-Aid from a glass jar—man, their kitchen pantry was a serious, huge walk-in. They had the best basement parties, whereas my grandma danced her you-know-what off. She was "dropping it like it's hot" before it became popular. While the 45s or vinyl albums played on the stereo, Grandma's dress hiked up, showing her knee-highs with knots on each outer end of the stockings. All the adults were dancing, drinking spirits, and having good old family fun.

As far as the religious aspect is concerned, they were Baptists. Grandma was a nurse at her church, wearing her white dress, white Oxford shoes, and that white nurse's hat. My granddad was kind of quiet, but a fun-loving patriarch who drank his Johnny Walker Red liquor. They also had some musical innuendos, but sports were their mantra. Softball was the dominant kingpin in that family. My grandparents had three sons, of which my dad was the middle son. Of course, all the brothers played softball. They were so good at it and well-recognized in the streets of Arthur Capper, Stonewall, and some others. My uncles and cousins have kept up that sports trait and mania to this day. Oh, and I forgot to mention that we have Proctor's Heritage in our blood on my paternal side.

CHAPTER 2

The Beginning of My Family

My parents attended public schools in the District of Columbia. Mom went to Saint Cyprian Catholic Elementary; Lovejoy; Terrell Junior High and graduated from Dunbar High School. Dad attended Van Ness Elementary, Randall Junior High, and graduated from Phelps Vocational High School. My mom told me she was a home-bound girl who loved to cook and bake. In high school, Mom also played the piano and danced ballet. It shocked me to learn that my mother wanted to become a policewoman, but worked for the Postal Service instead. There are numerous photos—some I snatched for my personal collection—of my mother and her worldly collection of fancy dresses and outfits. They were gorgeous and elegant. The trim-lined dresses and pencil skirts. The knee-high pedal pushers or knickerbockers looked good on her.

Dad was sort of an introvert who wore khakis most of the time. In school, he was into his sports. While attending Phelps Vocational School, his trade was an electrician, and he was good at it. In which he carried that knowledge into the Air Force. In school, baseball was his only passion as he played first base softball.

His all-time favorites were old Western movies, some sci-fi, black, and white movies, combat movies, comedies like Redd Fox and Moms Mabley, and boxing. We both watched boxing matches together, but he enjoyed watching the Washington Commanders (formerly The Redskins) without any company. I remember evenings of us eating hard-boiled eggs while watching *The Muppets* or movies such as *Arsenic and Old Lace*, *Blondie and Dagwood*, and any Betty Davis movies. However, I could not get into the old Western movies.

Dad honorably retired as a Veteran of the United States Air Force. What I did not know was that he had received a pass just to come home and marry my mom. Then, he had to deport back to Germany. Talk about true dedication and love. During his term in the service, the Air Force was going to pay for him to attend softball camp, but my mother did not want to raise me and my sisters by herself, nor wanted him to be away again for a long time, so it didn't happen. I've always wondered if he would have become a professional player.

CHAPTER 3

Family Life

From this union, five children were born: four daughters (rest in heaven, baby sister) and one son. If I may be sarcastic for a moment: I was the talented, beautiful, loving middle child. We were not rich, but we were not wealthy either. My parents were blue-collar, middle-class working status quo. So, we were living comfortably. Mom made sure we had a full-course meal for dinner throughout the entire week. The weekends were fast food and TV dinners. In the winter, the weekend's favorite meals were bean and ham soup and, are you ready? *Pig feet* drowned in vinegar and hot sauce with coleslaw…yum, yum. Mom did not bake from scratch, but her Betty Crocker box cakes were so delicious and moist just using the basic ingredients with a tab of vanilla extract. Her cakes were never dry at all, considering. Everyone knew about our kitchen pantry. Mom kept it fully stocked with goodies, candy, and doughnuts. I'm glad we did not become diabetics with all those sweets. Even our friends came over sometimes to eat dinner and/or have some type of dessert. Our door was always open.

Surprisingly, neither of my parents drove or had a vehicle. We relied on my maternal grandfather to take us everywhere, as I mentioned in the previous chapter. He was extremely patient, or at least he appeared to be. Granddad drove us to the grocery stores, school, and even the malls. Oh man, we could close a mall up, but he found a bench and patiently waited for us. I used to get scared when the stores started turning off lights and closing their roll-up doors. I thought we were going to get left inside and must sleep overnight. I remember always getting excited when we were going to the big-time Landover Mall in Landover, Maryland. It was a brand-new brick-and-mortar mall, so that was the place to go back then. I will admit that I committed my first do-or-dare at that mall. My sister dared me to snatch a halter top from the rack. I did and was successful. I was so scared afterward, and it never happened again. Thank goodness they did not have cameras set up yet. I think I repented when going to confession in grade school, so do not judge me (smile).

Even though my parents came from two different religious upbringings, we did not have the luxury of making our own decisions. My siblings and I became Catholics. Catholic elementary, Catholic high school, and, of course, attended Holy Comforter—St. Cyprian Catholic Church.

The Seven Holy Sacraments were a crucial part of our lives: Baptism (Holy water and Holy oils), Confirmation

(Chrismation/Christian initiation for anointing and giving a Holy name), Holy Eucharist (the bread and wine), Reconciliation (not to steal—repent), Anointing of the Sick (anointed oil for the sick and shut-in); Holy Orders (given to Christian males to become a deacon, priest, and bishop), and Holy Matrimony (marriage with a catholic ceremony).

CHAPTER 4

Reminiscing

Out of the daughters, I was the tomboy of the trio. My two older sisters were all about their boyfriends, friends, and concerts. Back then, Barbie dolls and paper dolls were a hit. I accumulated a slew of the original Malibu Barbies and her entourage—Ken, Skipper, PJ, and more. Each Christmas, I got a new item for them. The Barbie cars, the camper, and plenty of doll clothes, of which I used an old suitcase to accommodate. My neighbors used to get mad at me when I didn't come outside to play. The dolls gave me enough entertainment. My vivid sense of make-believe was out of this world. When the Barbie dolls had parties (like really), I used the tall, white plastic salt and pepper shakers as their cousins. I was super creative and loved it so much that I took my time going outdoors to play. My classmate and I made paper dolls and clothes.

The new millennials don't have a clue about making it work and being creative.

However, when I did go outdoors, the tomboy behavior came out. Our house was a row house, with plenty of kids around the neighborhood. Directly across the street is Chamberlain Vocational High School ball field, which today is an elementary charter school. Every time the boys in the neighborhood played baseball, they always selected me to be on their team. This sunny evening, as my dad sat on the porch watching us play ball, as he always did, it was my turn to hit the ball. Well surprisingly, I hit the ball, and it went over the fence—*home run!* I saw him stand up, proud and tall. Hell, I could not believe it myself. *I had a voice.* This made me immensely popular, and that became a big ordeal with the guys. That gave them the notion of always selecting me on their team. Also, I remember walking with my dad to Watkins Park in Southeast. When I was much younger, he put me on his shoulders because the walk was too exhausting when attending his softball games. Either I watched him play on his team, the Saints, or we watched other teams play. My dad and his brothers, uncles, and cousins were always there as well. It was like a family affair out there. They played in several tournaments there, Arthur Capper and Stonewalls. My father's youngest brother was a fast pitcher, and everyone knew him and his talent.

My dad and my siblings would walk in the southeast neighborhood of Capitol Hill on Halloween nights. Remember those plastic masks and the outfits? Sometimes, we were creative and designed our costumes. By the end of the night, our bags were full of candy, fruits, and even money. Yes, people dropped loose coins in my Halloween bag.

Football was another sport I engaged in, but was not fond of it. With both of my gender friends, we played dodgeball, kickball, high-low, and racing. Talk about a daredevil—I would jump off certain ledges, depending on the height. In my elementary school, there was a door from the auditorium that went outside to the playground. Well, in my Catholic school uniform jumper, I went up the exterior steps, climbed over the rail, and jumped down to the playground. Never once did I get hurt. I didn't know that all these radical moves were preparing me to become the firefighter that I am.

Then there was my musical side. As a young girl, I expressed an interest in playing the piano. Again, remember that my grandfather drove me to school and picked me up almost every day. My older two sisters were in high school at St. Cecilia's Academy. That afternoon, picking me up from my school was different. In my grandfather's Lincoln were my grandmother and uncle. It never dawned on me what was about to happen. So, when we got to my house and as I entered, my parents were in the living room, along with a brand-spanking-new piano. It was black lacquer in color. The piano had an emblem in the middle that read: Baldwin. That was a huge surprise as I smiled from ear to ear. I was told that my uncle paid for me to take piano lessons. The piano studio was on U Street Northwest—the studio placard is still on the front exterior house today. My playtime in the evenings ceased because of piano lessons and practicing at home. My piano instructor was an older lady that carried a thin wooden stick. She sometimes fell asleep while I played my assigned lesson for her. I learned my lessons on her baby grand piano. Well, this one particular evening, I called myself being a smarty pants. She had fallen asleep, so I thought, so I played the wrong notes. Lo-and-behold, that stick whacked across my knuckles. She was sleeping but listening. She did not have to worry about me underestimating her again. She made sure my posture and poise were straight. I had to position my hands and wrist in their proper piano placements. I was given assignments from Sherwood Music School and she freaking graded me on them and turned them in. Then there were the piano recitals. My parents, grandparents, and uncle were always there to support me. I don't think my sisters attended—lucky them. At one recital, I dressed as Hiawatha as I played an Indian song. At another recital, I played "Swan Lake" and did very well. This continued until around the age of twelve, as I was entering pre-teens. I felt like this was a little girl's hobby and therefore I quit, in which I regret quitting today. Outside was calling my name and the boys. As they say, "You're smelling yourself."

Growing up in my household, we had chores: washing dishes, and we better had sweep the kitchen floor afterwards. One easy chore that I did hate was taking down the fresh-smelling clothes off the clothesline out back with those wooden clothespins. Another chore was we kept our bedroom straight and dusted. We never had to mop or clean the toilet, though, thank goodness. Well, if we went out or stayed up late on Fridays, the chores still had to be done in the morning. Remember earlier, I mentioned my dad was in the military? Dad woke up early, even on the weekends. On Saturdays, I remember waking up as he was being loud and didn't care if we were still asleep. So, you had no choice but to wake up. Sometimes, on our combined stereo/radio set downstairs, he played the United States Air Force Symphony Orchestra album on that stereo/radio combo set—hated it. Sometimes, I felt like waking up to march around my room just to clean up. He even gave me a US Air Force Symphony album for my birthday one year, and all I could do was smile, but under my breath, I was like, "Really?" As that day went on, his genre of music changed. It went from B.B. King to James Brown to, finally, if you can believe it, Chuck Brown. My mom sometimes played R&B 45s—Aretha Franklin, Marvin Gaye, The Dells, Gladys Knight and the Pips, and much more. This contributed to my love of old songs, and I knew the lyrics to them. Our household had fun times.

As I explored the outdoors more and boys, Dad noticed it as well. I gradually let go of the tomboyish antics and slowly embraced girlhood. Every time a new male appeared around our way to play whatever we were playing, Dad came on the porch and embarrassingly asked, "Who is that clown,

13

and where did he come from?" How I hated it when he did this, but not realizing this was his way of protection. Hell, he had three girls to contend with, along with three different personalities.

CHAPTER 5

Siblings

"A man prepares his plans and thoughts from the heart, but the answer he is given comes from the Lord. All man's ways may seem right in their eyes, but God examines all motives commit to him and your plans will succeed." For God is the Alpha and the Omega.

— Proverbs 16:1-3

Our household had fun times. We also had difficult times. When my little sister was born, our lives changed. She was the baby of the bunch. I was told that my maternal grandmother was the one who noticed her gait was not normal. We would sit her up on the sofa and she would automatically lean over to her side. Being a naïve schoolgirl, I thought nothing of it. I just thought as a baby she was not ready to sit up yet. However, she always remained a jolly, happy little girl like any other baby.

Years later, we all had to take a neurological test. I was so afraid that my dad had to come into the room when it was my turn. I vaguely remember being hooked up to wiring probes. When they waved an instrument over the nerves, they would flex and pulsate. Boy, that felt so eerie; it made my skin crawl, not knowing that's what it was supposed to do. My baby sister was diagnosed with Muscular Dystrophy. As a young girl, she did everything as someone without a disability. Those brown braces did not stop her from dancing, playing, and being a normal child. However, things changed after she had to endure serious, extensive surgery to install a rod into her back. This became somewhat of a setback for her and our family. We were all devastated and hurt. This became heavy on my parents as the medical bills were coming in, and I saw the worry and stress on them, but we survived it. That was how she became spoiled because everyone showered her with love.

My little sister lived a normal life. She had a boyfriend who did not mind pushing her in her wheelchair to ride the subway. They would go on little dates to the movies, amusement parks, and the beach. She was a smart, well-dressed teen and kept all the latest hairstyles. She went to her prom and even had a handicapped-equipped vehicle. She went on her first cruise with my family and Dad's side of the family. My girl graduated from Roosevelt High School in Northwest Washington, DC as the salutatorian. From there, she worked at the Department of Agriculture until her death in March 2020. My parents made sure she had the world. The *love* our parents had for us was impeccable, unconditional *love*.

My two older sisters were into their own thing with school and dating. My oldest sister was dating her boyfriend-turned-husband (rest in heaven). My pre-brother-in-law became my chauffeur. He drove me to weekend dances and patiently picked me up. Hell, he was my chauffeur to my eleventh-grade prom. When I had permission to have a teen basement party, of course, he and his buddies were the chaperones. Such good times.

Back to my sister. She loved her music. She had the front bedroom all to herself, which was passed down to us all after one moved. I remember always entering her room and listening to her style of music. What a genre of albums. We listened to Earth, Wind & Fire, Santana, Rare Earth, Minnie Riperton, AWB, Hall and Oates, and too many to list. She even played artists such as David Bowie, Tower of Power, and Sir Elton John. I knew all the lyrics to "Bennie and the Jets." because of her.

My other sister was into music as well. She introduced me to live concerts. I went to almost all the live entertainment with her and her then-boyfriend. I was the third wheel, or as they say, "the tag-along sister." I would keep the other end of all my tickets and put it in my personal album book (everybody had that old picture binder that had the sticky back to it to hold the tickets). The best part was that they did not mind me going with them. Well, the very first memorable concert I attended with them was the infamous, electrifying, funksters Parliament Funkadelic with George Clinton at the well-known Capitol Center in Landover, Maryland. OMG! The things they did back in those days at that arena. Well, being naïve, I had no clue until that evening. Man, the parking lot was full of cars. As we entered the arena, folks were everywhere. You couldn't walk a foot without bumping into someone. They were lollygagging, buying souvenirs or food. As we were walking to find our seats, I noticed a huge, thick haze in the air. Perplexed, I still did not have a clue. Well, as soon as we got to our seats, who had gotten sick? I told them I felt dizzy and sick to my stomach. Damn, damn, damn. I had gotten a contact. That haze was from the residues of marijuana that hovered inside the entire arena. It angered my sister because we had just gotten there, and the concert had not even started yet. So, her boyfriend had to take me outside to get some fresh air. (It's funny now looking back). After sucking up as much air as possible, he got me some food. I was good to go or probably still high. Who knows? Let the concert begin.

Thanks to Parliament Funkadelic, I discovered my serious love of live music and the sounds of different instruments. The bass guitar player was so intense and heavy that I swear it made my shirt rumble. The costumes were out of this world, but the stage and pyrotechnical props were unbelievable. The mothership hung from the ceiling and landed on the stage.

The trap door opened and out came Parliament Funkadelic. I was in awe. On stage, the performers were even smoking blunts. I have never forgotten that show and the good, loud music. Because of that, all other live shows I attended had to come correctly, especially with the bass guitar. Other concerts that matched were The Brother Johnsons and Slave, to name a few (it was so many to name). Rick James, Kool & the Gang (with that electrifying synthesizer), The Commodores and so many more had me enjoying other instruments such as horns and the piano, as well as their voices. Their sound had to be precise and clear for me to enjoy. I depicted every instrument sound at Sade's concerts as she glided across the stage like a mermaid. I saw Patti LaBelle at the Capitol Center, too. Her vocals were so towering that I thought she was about to crack the lenses on my glasses. She has high-pitched vocals. I saw Tina Turner, and that was a serious female rockstar concert, to say the least. My ear for music got so good that I could sometimes tell if something was off or as I say, "It sounds cheap." I thought I was going to go to college to become an audio engineer because I studied the concert engineer's moves as they always sat in the middle of the arena, controlling the sounds. So as an adult, my love for music, loud music, and all instruments started when I was a young'un.

My only brother—poor thang—did boy things and got whooping's. We had the switch that was always near my dad in the back room of our house, stationed atop the window fan. Speaking of fans, Dad truly believed in having the fan blow out to draw out the hot air in the house. Boy, did we sweat. Back to my brother, who I remember had mouthed off to my mother and she let him have it, and it even scared me. The one thing that stood out was that he had a healthy appetite. He was such a husky-built fella that, in high school, some of my friends thought he was a football player. However, he was quiet, or at least in my eyes. He also had a love for music, especially the well-known genre of go-go that is popular in the Washington, DC, Maryland, and Virginia (also known as the DMV) areas. Local groups like Rare Essence,

Ayre Rayde, and the Soul Train Award Winning, Grammy-nominated Experience Unlimited with Sugar Bear took the world by storm with their single, "Da Butt," which the group performed in Spike Lee's movie, *School Daze*. Since we both enjoyed go-go, how could he not be a Chuck Brown fan like me?

Going to the movies was a part of my life as well. I enjoyed horror movies and comedies. However, the two main flicks that had me scared were the original *Dracula* and, of course, *The Exorcist*. After seeing *Dracula*, it had me hallucinating with bats flying around my head. So, I yelled for my mother to come here because I could not sleep. She was mad and scolded me not to see any more fictional crap movies. Did I listen? Not! However, *The Exorcist*—I knew I was not about to see that. My bestie and her sister saw it and told me some scenes. Again, scared out of my wits, but I damn sure was not about to wake up my mother again. I could not even watch the movie when it came out on television for a good while. Especially when they mentioned the infamous external stairs in Georgetown. This movie had lots of folks frightened. However, this did not stop me from seeing *Blacula, Amityville Horror, Friday the 13th, Phantasm, Texas Chainsaw Massacre*, and many more.

Life is a biorhythm of components: ups and downs, predictable and unpredictable circumstances, the divergence of man and woman, and fire and its temperamental components to sustain combustion. Education is essential to teach us and to reach us.

Colleges and universities provide for that pivotal degree; physicians become educated to give the best medical expertise; Christianity, whether a priest, rabbi, pastor, or deacon, exemplifies theological practices and views. However, God; Allah; Jehovah; Adonai, and Yahweh have the final—ultimate—definitive, fervent calling and power of it **ALL.**

CHAPTER 6

My First Health Scare

"As Jesus set out on a tour of all the cities and villages, teaching in their synagogues preaching the good news of his word and curing every sort of disease and every sort of infirmity."

– Matthew 9:35

On September 30, 1962, at Georgetown University Hospital, a beautiful Libran was born at 3:19 a.m. From the circa photos, I was a healthy, good-sized, bubbly baby. Toddler years began with wearing hard white or brown Oxford walking shoes, and hair in several plaits with ribbons or bows. The hard oxford shoes remind me of those shoes with a corrective bar at the bottom. So glad I did not have cub feet. My mother always dressed me and my two sisters in the same outfits—I did the same with my three daughters when they were young. The black patent leather shoes with the satin ruffled ankle socks seemed like a standard toddler uniform. Cute sundresses with matching bonnets. I was adorable.

We lived comfortably in our two-bedroom apartment on K Street Southeast. Life went on as normal for me and my family. Until that health scare snuck into our home and my life. I can only remember certain health scare events because I was just a toddler—a terribly ill toddler.

That cute, chubby little girl became a whittle, fragile toddler. My parents gradually noticed I had stopped playing with my toys and lost my appetite. House doctors were the physicians back then. They were given that jargon because their office was located inside their private residence. Well, my parents took me to this physician. However, I was not improving at all. My weight had diminished from being healthy to thin. My fever continued to spike, especially at night. My father used to always phrase the old wives' tale that "After sunset, all your illnesses come out." Well, there is truth to that saying. It seemed like my fever would spike at night. I couldn't keep anything down, not even water. Another wise medical approach was the use of raw onions. My paternal grandmother chopped up raw onions and placed them in a handkerchief (I do remember that). She placed the onion concoction on both wrists to break my spiked fever. With all those home remedies, I felt like I was being prepped to be in a veggie salad. I believe it helped somewhat, but not sure if she put the raw onions in my socks at night. However, I thought I was getting better and tried some of the red Kool-Aid my sister had made for us—that was the main kid drink back then—but that didn't hold up. Everything I consumed caused me to violently projectile, as the fever never left.

One day at my maternal grandmother's house, I was told that I looked very limp as I lay on the sofa. My father was so upset and concerned that he said, "We must take her out of here." So, Grandma found another house physician that evening and was told to get me there ASAP. Of course, my grandfather drove us there. The physician said I was dreadfully ill and whoever that other physician was, he was giving me the wrong medication to help me. I still do not know if I had viral hepatitis or not. However, I was truthfully told that if my parents had not gotten a second opinion, I would have had a few months to live. The thought of losing a child from a healthy state to almost death—I can only imagine how it took a toll on my entire family tree.

After getting some information on my illness from my aunt for this autobiography, she said I was tangibly ill, and my fragile appearance did not look good at all. Everyone feared the worst. However, God had plans for me that, as a toddler, I had no clue about. I was too young to know God, but He knew me. With the new medication given and other medical procedures, I slowly got better. My appetite was still very bleak, but it was coming back. My recollection was my laying on the sofa with my dad, looking at the tv while eating PB&J sandwiches and drinking RC Colas. I enjoyed reading my "Highlights" magazines as well. Later in my growing years, all my close friends knew I loathed peanut butter and jelly sandwiches—this was how it started. This food regime was my favorite until I started maneuvering to other foods, which was probably how my enjoyment of dark sodas got started. Other family members kept in close contact, following my health improvement. My dad's cousin always visited me as my strength improved. I recall those days when we would sit in the dining area, listening to my Close 'n Play Phonograph. I remember looking at old Westerns with Dad while still eating my PB&J sandwiches. Eventually, my health improved to where I was ready to go to preschool at Watkins and Buchanan before entering Catholic elementary school.

As Mom would pick me up from my early childhood schooling, we would go to Johnny Boys to get those delectable hot smoking ribs. My appetite had returned, but without the weight gain, though. Well, I was ready to enter grade school. Catholic School is first through eighth grade. The Oblate Sisters of Providence were practically most of our teachers and they did not play. This is where I met my two best friends, as we are still friends. First grade was my first boy crush. I felt like a normal girl, and without allowing my small frame to hinder me. I recall days when my principal would make sure I had some type of fruit at lunchtime. Some kids thought I was the principal's pet, but they did not know the reason behind my nutritional status. Peanut butter and jelly sandwiches had upgraded to Mom's famous tuna sandwiches.

As years went by, I was back into a normal routine as

a kid. Remember from the previous chapters, I exemplified myself as a tomboy and a girl. The normal childhood illnesses I got. My friends could attest to that every time we received that school booster shot, or caught a cold, and even played outside in the snow—Mom would give us aspirin and/or those nasty-tasting laxatives...ugh. The childhood candies: Boston Baked Beans, Lemonheads, Red Hots, Jawbreakers, Alexander the Grape, and my favorite: Chico Sticks.

Mom worked the night shift at the post office, but when she got home, she checked on us all. When I got sick, she would always come into my bedroom and rub me down with that green or clear rubbing alcohol, saying it helped keep the fever down. My parents were the bomb parents to all of us.

I was a studious child that got decent grades as I entered middle scholastics. Every summer, I had that good old DC Summer Youth Employment Program, founded by former Washington, DC, Mayor Marion Barry. I held jobs at different recreational centers. When filling out the job application, a birth certificate and proof of being a District of Columbia resident were standard. This was when I discovered our family's intimate blessing. I never paid much attention to the details on my birth certificate until one day I noticed the written verbiage of asking how many children were living (two), how many other children were born alive but are deceased (zero), and how many children were stillborn (one). From the past to the present, my methodical intuition had declared my sister, even though it does not state the sex, as my spiritual deliverance and guardian angel throughout my entire life. Knowing this placed a special bond in my heart that I will carry until we meet. Note: my mother gave permission to release this personal family information.

Back to my summer job. I had a little spending money of my own, and it felt good. I felt grown and mature. Throughout the remaining school years, I received the Sacrament of Confirmation being anointed by the oil of Chrism. This is when you get a Biblical Catholic name to be your evangel protector. My Confirmation name is Elizabeth derivative: Elizabeth Ann Seton was the first Canonized female declared as a Saint by the Roman Catholic Church. Later, I had been voted upon and selected as The May Queen at the May

Procession. This is also a Catholic tradition, honoring Mother Mary Magdalene's coronation and crowning of her blessed statue. But the highlight of my grade school was entering eighth grade. This was an exciting timeframe for us all as we selected our high school. Commencement day had finally arrived. I graduated with honors. My favorite graduation gift was a bushel of crabs. *Yum!* Of course, we also ate at the once-famous Chesapeake Bay Seafood House, which stayed crowded. Everything was so normal and perfect as I prepared to enter high school at St. Cecilia's Academy in Southeast Washington, DC. I felt grown. Until that summer.

CHAPTER 7

Here We Go Again

L ife was going well for me. I had a slew of friends from school and in the neighborhood. I finally was easing up on the boyish ways as I was experiencing female puberty and its role. However, I continued to wear jeans all the time and could not adjust to skirts, heels, or makeup. Not yet anyway. This evening should have been a normal repetitive evening: being outdoors, eating dinner, and later taking a bath. While taking my bath in my personal little world, my mother came into the bathroom to get something. There, she noticed something on my upper back. She then called my dad to come and look. Scared, yes, but I did not know what was going on. I knew it had to be serious, though, when she summoned my dad. They said my back looked uneven and described it as a lump growing on one side.

At the doctor's appointment, we learned I had a fatty tumor growing at the upper left side of my poor little back that needed to be removed. Did I need anything else to happen to me? Hell no, but as you continue to read the rest of my story; this is just the beginning.

Luckily, they scheduled my surgery during the summer. This was my very first hospitalization, and I hated it. On the day of surgery, I recall my mother and her brother were there with me. I did not forget the medicinal injection pierced into my little buttocks. Boy, I hollered like a frightened little girl acting like it was my first day of preschool. It was amazing as the years passed that I must look at every injection given to me, even when they draw blood from me. Then, they had the nerve to put the IV in my arm with the old fashion arm board (splint) attached and tightly secured for immobilization. I remember a drainage tube coming from my back into the drainage bag. My hospitalization was for a few days. Within those days, my dad visited and brought my *Mad* magazines to read. I finally received my discharge papers and home instructions. Why? Because I had a slew of stitches on my back.

Little by little, my life got back to normal. I could even go outside for a while, mainly on the porch. Until one day an incident happened, and that tomboy came out—or as they say, the Souf East- slang for southeast came out. I was in a fight and loosened some of my stitches. My parents were livid. Hell, I was, too, because I could not fathom getting more stitches again. After that occurrence, I had to stay indoors for a while. Then, when I eventually went back outside, it was porch games such as jacks (I was a pro) and uno cards. I had to get my act together because high school would be calling my name soon.

Still not recognizing my guardian angels had accompanied me along the way with my blessings, along with my voice.

CHAPTER 8

The Joys of Female Adolescence

Saint Cecilia Academy accepted my transcript. When I attended Catholic high school, the grades were ninth through twelfth. This was an all-girls high school, which was a whole new environment for me. No more granddaddy to drive me to school as I either walked or took the #32 bus route. I was starting to physically and mentally blossom. Getting my haircut and permed to wearing an old brown stocking with the knot on top at night as my hair cap; wearing just a pinch of makeup—that I somehow licked the lipstick off all the time—and slowly getting away from wearing Jordache, Gloria Vanderbilt, Levi's or Sassoon jeans.

Attending an all-girls high school was very questionable. Yuck—zero males, prepare for fights, jealousy, cliques, and so on. Despite those negative ideologies, I was excited to go because I was evolving. My life was transforming into young, female adulthood.

As a freshman, I had to select a big sister who was an upper-class girl who was supposed to guide me throughout. I had the best big sister that was assigned to me. However, other upper-class girls looked after me as well. And then there was the brother school: Mackin, an all-boys Catholic high school. They could only attend our school for sock hops or basketball games, and vice versa. They were awesome. I met some boys there, but I was kind of shy, so I kept to myself. Learning is fundamental and despite some cutups, I remained a studious gal.

There was an honors assembly, of which I received an award. I did not know the school had called my family to witness my becoming an honor student inducted into the Honor Society. I was thrilled to see my family there. It was a goal of mine with the determination to remain in the honors society. At Saint Cecilia Academy, I was involved in many extra-curriculum activities at school—the drill team, National Honor Society, drama club, and talent shows. My very first well-known play was depicted from *For Colored Girls Who Have Considered Suicide / When the Rainbow Is Enuf* written by the legendary Ntozake Shange. Such a deep and meaningful choreography of life in stories and poems.

We even dressed in colorful leotards and flowing skirts to match. My color was black. Our drama teacher was the coolest instructor I had ever met. She took us to Arena Stage in Southwest to introduce us to live stage plays. Maybe my niche was acting because I thought I was good at it.

Then there was the driver's education class given at a public school. I remember going to there and riding in the car with other students. The instructor had to get on me because my foot hit the gas pedal like I was a female NASCAR driver. Then behold, the learner's permit to driver's license was an immeasurable feeling of blessings: conquistador. Upper-class girls hear me roar. I met and became friends with several girls at my high school, whom I still stay in touch with or hang out with today.

CHAPTER 9

Trying to be Grown

Yes, it was finally here: PROM TIME. I had a so-called boyfriend or just a crush. I remember writing notes to boys, asking: Do you like me, yes or no? Do you want to have a chance, yes or no? Dang, at that age, we were giving each other options. Well, I did not want him to take me to my junior prom. After several of my girlfriends and I decided we wanted to have a really good time without being stuck beside a dude, we all went solo. I had the best time ever as I danced the night away. My infamous brother-in-law was our chauffeur. Experience Unlimited was our band group along with a deejay. However, seeing other girls with dates had me feeling some kind of way. Still, I had so much fun with my girls that the conviction of having a date vanished, especially when some girls with dates just sat at the table or took pictures. While the band took their break, the deejay spun a favorite tune of mine, and, boy, did I dance up a sweat. "Holy Ghost" by the Barclays. As Big Momma, played by

Martin Lawrence in *Big Momma's House*, said, "That's my jam!"

From 1979 to 1980, I became a high school senior. Pre-adulthood, here I come. Drinking Pink and Golden Champale and even trying to be grown smoking cigarettes; I felt sick to my stomach, smoking one cigarette. I never touched the stick again. Also was the introduction to the "nickel bag marijuana (aka reefer) as I smoked a joint here and there but glad that was a phase in my adolescence that came and left. I'm sure I'm not alone in saying that I couldn't wait to grow up. If only I had a crystal ball or a good psychic to tell me, "Yes, you can wait."

I studied hard, and got good grades, as I filled out paperwork to help me enter college. Back then, the schools had the stay-in work-study program. Other students worked at other various government agencies that offered that program. I, along with some of my girlfriends, worked part-time at the Department of Justice in Northwest. We worked full-time during the holidays and summer. Working at a real job and receiving my own pay felt empowering. This also introduced me to the foundation of work etiquette while working with adults. With my charming personality, I became friends with some of those adults and met their wives/girlfriends and both. I was the daughter or little sister. They treated me to some delectable lunches in which Johnny Boy fast food carryout was our favorite. I would get a slab of ribs and eat them all to myself. (still didn't gain any weight).

Then there was senior prom. This time I had a date. He was my high school crush. So, my appearance had to be on point—hair done; nails done. Yes, I had to be fancy like the song says. He had a car, too. Of course, my parents met him as I met his parents, so it was all copacetic. After prom was the after party, so we dashed to The Crystal City Underground Club in Crystal City, Virginia. Afterwards, came graduation day. All Catholic high school graduations took place at the National Shrine on Michigan Avenue, Northeast. Circa 1980 was my senior graduation of approximately sixty-plus seniors. The University of Maryland Eastern Shore, here I come. *Not!*

The "how-to" or "what to do" for the financial side of going to college was not fully or properly explained to my parents. That phone call, one spring day, broke my educational high. A guidance counselor had called the house to state that I was going to be roommates with one of my girlfriends from high school. I was excited and elated until my father stated, "Thanks, but she will not be attending. We do not have the financial means for her to attend." Broken-hearted, crying, and angry was all I could perceive out of all of this. Why didn't anyone tell me about their decision? Maybe we could have figured something out. So, my dreams of becoming an RN were shot down. I feel like my parents didn't have the right guidance when it came to financing my college education.

Instead of letting this hold me back, I enrolled at the University of the District of Columbia for nursing, but only in the LPN Program. There, I met another girlfriend. As we grew into a friendship and bonded, I found out that her mother attended the same church: Holy Comforter Church. The LPN program consisted of different levels. I was in nursing II and could not wait for nursing III, which was OB/GYN. Nursing level III was only offered in the springtime with clinicals at the famous teaching hospital, DC General. Of course, to advance to the next level, I had to pass the exams. Well, nursing II had a lot of math (the metric system). I had to learn the old-school method of using the metric system to determine the drops per minute (gtts/ml) calculation formula for the IV drop flow rate. My fear of math allowed it to consume me so badly that I failed the math section on IV drops per minute. Devastation and hurt again were calling my name. I could not attend nursing level III until the following springtime. Because of my anger, I quit nursing school instead of taking other courses. My newfound girlfriend from UDC was distraught as well. However, we made a promise that she would graduate for me. She kept her promise and became a registered nurse. Today, she is a traveling RN and doing well.

CHAPTER 10

Continuing My Education

"No temptation has come upon you except what is common to men. But God and only God is faithful, as he will not let you be tempted beyond what you can bear, but along with that temptation he will also make the way out so that you may be able to endure it."

— 1 Corinthians 10:13

With my passion and determination for healthcare, I was determined to find my niche. I was accepted into The Georgetown Medical Assistant Program. This engaged me in the health profession as well as meeting new confidants. Two of my classroom divas became long-lasting friends. I remember learning how to do injections on a nice juicy orange until we finally had to do our partners. Whew, child! But we got the job done. I didn't realize this medical field was preparing me for the much bigger picture. I graduated and received my certificate. I became a certified medical assistant.

In 1987, my first medical employment was working for two medical internists.

When the practice moved to a medical building on M Street, Northwest, two things occurred to me. One, I was doing the job of a registered nurse, giving injections, performing EKGs, and phlebotomy, and assisting with sigmoidoscopies. The only thing I did not do was IVs. Second, my boss, who was a primary care physician, had a lot of high-end patients. My performance got noticed, and they compensated for it. One incident caused me to get a raise. This patient had been in the hospital for health reasons in which the phlebotomist had bruised her arm trying to locate the veins. After I did my scope of work meaning taking vitals, EKG, the doctor came in and said he would draw her blood because of the small veins. However, she stated I could give it a try.

So, while they were in deep conversation, I plucked and plucked, balling her fist, slapping that forearm like it was a child getting a beating. Then I took the gauge needle and inserted it into her vein. The room got incredibly quiet. The blood flowed into the tubes, which were labeled as getting a CBC-complete blood count. This patient immediately said, "Doc, give her a raise," and I got my raise. She was a descendant of the Dupont family, known for their Dupont Paint. After that, I was on cloud nine and ten. That short time I attended nursing school had prepared me for it all.

That was why it disappointed my boss when I left his practice in 1989.

CHAPTER 11

My Wedding Bliss: Another Setback Only For a Positive Comeback

L ove was in the air, for sure. Dating my high school sweetheart was impeccable, at least I thought so. We were inseparable. We knew everything about each other's likes/dislikes, food, entertainment, etc. He knew when I was down or stressed from nursing school with studying. He would bring me a small token to cheer me up, such as my favorite pineapple upside-down cake or homemade shrimp egg foo young with gravy, and down to the smallest token of buying grape BUBBLE YUM, which was my favorite. Oh, did I mention he was a chef? Every other Friday was our movie date and Chinese food. Sometimes, I used to get somewhat afraid because the relationship seemed too perfect. This man had the utmost respect for me, considering we both were young in our early twenties. Everyone knew us as *that couple*, including the physicians I worked for. I bragged about him as he bragged about me. Wow! When he purchased his first car, he came right over to my parents' house to give me a set of keys. He said no more public transportation or borrowing his family member's car to take me or us places. That high school crush turned into true love for a couple of years for us.

In my early twenties, I was in a plethora of weddings— whether as a bridesmaid or a guest. Every woman dreams of having a wonderland, beautiful, blissful wedding day. And it finally was going to happen for me. At least I thought so. That evening we enjoyed the night out as he made reservations to stay overnight at a hotel. There, he proposed to me with an engagement ring in his hand. A dream come true. I was finally getting married. Everyone was extremely excited for us— his male friends and, of course, my girlfriends. I was finally going to be a bride and not a bridesmaid. I was floating on a cloud. "Heaven must be like this."

Wedding plans were in the makings. We reserved the church—even though he was not Catholic. I had a large wedding party consisting of my girlfriends because I did not want to leave anyone out. Six or seven bridesmaids and groomsmen. I selected a white puffy wedding gown. It was lavish with lots of ruffles and satin shoes. I had chosen lilac for the bridesmaids. To show my sincere friendship and gratitude, I had their dresses custom-made, and I incurred all the expenses. They had their satin shoes dyed lilac to complement their gowns. Things were moving right along and in place.

We both had good stable jobs and income for youngsters. Did I tell you we even purchased a home in Temple Hills, Maryland? We became first-time home buyers. So, who could not ask for more? Selecting furniture and home décor like grown folks; I even had my dad inspect the home. I learned a lot of lessons regarding homeownership, especially before I became a fire inspector. One was a flat roof, which was a no-go. He also pointed out a few other home impediments we had to adjust. Nevertheless, it was a wonderful feeling. With the wedding date set, I mailed the invitations out.

Little did I expect the unexpected.

What a majestic, sunny day that was picture-perfect, my one and only called me to say we needed to talk, and he would come by to pick me up. I could tell by his voice something was not quite right. Mom was in the kitchen preparing dinner and talking on the phone when I informed her, I would be right back. Once I got inside our car—his car—the atmosphere was tense and uncomfortable. I kept asking, "What is going on?" He stated he wanted to ride to a park to talk. As I saw tears forming in his eyes, it was no way that ride to the park was going to happen. I told him, "Pull over and *talk*."

Wham! A ton of bricks just hit me. My perfect little world just crashed.

The love of my life was not the love of my life after all. He cried as the words formed out of his mouth that he just could not get married.

"No, it's just cold feet and it will blow over," I said.

With overflowing tears streaming down his face, there was nothing I could have said that would have made a difference. I saw his hurt and pain, and my own. He constantly kept apologizing for hurting me.

All I could think was, *who wants to hear this? All these years of commitment and this? What am I going to do now?*

Dropping me off at my parents' house with eyes filled with tears, he grabbed my hand, but I recoiled. I slammed the car door, only to run inside the house.

My mother, who was still on the phone, turned around and yelled, "What's wrong with you?"

"My wedding is called off! He does not want to get married."

That beautiful sunny day became one of the dark, gloomiest days of my life. Little did I know that this was also a testament to my faith.

From my room, I heard my mother downstairs in shock as well. His grandmother called me to ask what was going on and said that he came home very upset. I told her what had transpired in a suffocating voice. "How can I tell everyone because this is unreal? Maybe if his family talks with him, then the wedding can still go on."

Granny called me a lot that day to continue to uplift me, as she was upset, too. She said he was hurting immensely. A few days later, my girlfriend's mother, my mom, and all called folks to let them know the wedding was called off. This was barely a three-week notification. This was only supposed to happen in the movies and not in real life. I remember my dad and close male cousins were so furious to the point of going over to his house. My bridesmaids were and still are loyal girlfriends. The church and the guests knew, but I was still in complete denial and pain and had become withdrawn.

The alleged wedding day finally arrived. It was a clear, crisp sunny afternoon that was picture-perfect. However, I was boarding the plane to Indiana with my bestie for the entire week. Her husband was in the military, and they had housing there. For that to have been my first plane ride, it was a ride of heartache—nothing is promising.

CHAPTER 12

I Found My Voice

DISSENSION

"God created man in his image; in God's image, he created a male and a female. God blessed them and said to them be fruitful and become many, fill the earth and subdue it."

– Genesis 1:27

TO SERVE WITH LOVE OR NOT:

Fool's gold of love and self-gratification—have we become a marginalized community? Society has stigmatized and/or acceptance of the definition of love, the new norm for love.

I am not an expert on the psychology/thesis of love. You love who you love. We all make mistakes in relationships, but don't let it define your character to the subjection of hate/ repugnancy, and you exhibit antagonism.

All creatures of life crave to be L O V E D: euphoria to romancing—that again started with the formation of Adam and Eve in the Garden of Eden and escalated to man and woman of today. Everyone wants to be loved in all forms of sexual orientations: woman, man, child, seniors, animals, etc. Loving who you want to love brings joy and freedom.

So, what is love? The essence of love is that special union bond of chemistry; teenage crush; a boo thing; highly strong endorphins; compatibility; getting out of the box; communication; love letters and picking out meaningful Hallmark cards; growth of endurance; smiles; gazing and grazing in the grass; trustworthiness; investment in marriage; that feeling of honor when your child/ren paid attention to you as they get older, being their superhero.

Love: supposed to validate oneself to ourselves that forms a union; lack of fear of being alone; high self-esteem that brings out those dormant emotions; listening to love songs; (those old school love songs had so many deep-rooted feelings, whether it was joy or pain) holding hands; wearing matching outfits; spiritually connected; pleasure principles with the understanding of constructive love and criticism; poetry; a beautiful melody; acceptance of appearance; acceptance of their lack of.

We learn that love is a beautiful metaphor of feelings (a rainbow of love colors). It's so colorful and powerful that sometimes we get lost.

Then L O V E can become the unimaginable—the lack of. The ray of sunshine turns into the rage of destructive storms.

Here comes the miscommunication, misinterpretations of each other; accusations big time; love turned to lust to greed (for the love of money); temptations in various forms; dehumanizing each other for the sake of self-worth; narcissism; grandiosity; idolization/premature feelings that led to disaster; plain old bored with each other—the lost identity.

Love idealization diminishes to where it becomes withdrawn, respect goes out the window on all accounts, or is there any respect at all?

The mind is there, but the heart left a long time ago, staying together for various reasons but miserable as hell.

In life, there are no guarantees. We love unconditionally, but do we really know the end results? Not even a crystal ball can dictate the scene. We do all we can for our loved ones. Even with our children, when they grow up, they have their own persona, and here comes the change; one becomes defiant, a criminal, an alcoholic, a gambler, lazy, successful, career-oriented; making money moves; millionaire, homebound with no ambitions, etc.

Love is blind; a fallacy that has become confusing and unpredictable. Everything appears to have become a condition (for some): stoic, emotionless drainage; love not to love—still waters do run deep and sometimes it is okay.

Recognize the five stages of dealing with love/hate: denial, anger, bargaining, depression, and finally acceptance.

It is a real human experience to fall in and out of love, but the key is conquering yourself foremost and not allowing defiance. This will prepare you for the next chapter—the next journey—the next love. And bring back God the Father in your life. Because it is obvious that He got lost in the mix and was not a priority.

Quote from the famous Michael Jackson: "The love you save may be your own."

Sometimes the inevitable resolution occurs that can help or hurt: And it is okay, sometimes even permissible:

Nothing But God, Our Lord and Savior whose Life and Love **For Us All** is UNCONDITIONAL and FORGIVING. So Why Can't We?

CHAPTER 13

Joy and Pain

My hostess, also my friend, made sure I felt loved. The days slowly became better for me, but was unsure once I returned home. There were a few wedding gifts left, and I was glad of that. I did not want to be reminded of that day. My physician boss and staff welcomed me back with open arms. He always had my back, as he called me into his office to express myself. He told me to always drink a shake with meals so I would not lose weight. Or to drink it to substitute eating on those gray days. And I did. Amazingly, no one could tell what I was going through at work. I continued to manage my patient care in the office. But once I got home, it was a different story. I had to force myself to eat dinner, and mom's dinners were the bomb. My bedroom was my safe refuge along with my phone. I would call my ex any time of the day or night and let him have it. All the explicit adjectives came rolling out of my mouth: the hurt, the anger, the devastation, and the humiliation. He allowed me to get it all out. He never hung up on me but only said, "I love you and I am sorry." I never paid attention to his suffering and why should I? Because it was a waste of money, time, and love. Dude, really?

One evening, I spoke to my girlfriend's mother (who treated me as her niece) on the phone. I have never forgotten her testimony of what she endured, but of how she overcame it. Her spoken words never left me. "God puts people in your life at certain times during certain seasons. And your pain is like a sore on your leg. If you keep picking at that sore, then how is it going to heal?" This resonated dearly as this started my healing. Of course, I heavily recited my prayers. Then, I let go and let God fully in. My nasty phone calls ceased, but only to listen. It opened my eyes, ears, and heart that he truly was aching. His friends even told me that this bulky, football physique-looking guy had lost weight and appeared to be in a dark place. I was told he would go to work and go straight home. Because the house we purchased was just a month old, it was easy to remove me from the obligations—he didn't keep it that long, anyway. I would ride past there, and it always looked dark, gloomy, and empty. He lived like a hermit. Female social cognitive is entirely different from our male counterparts. Our traits display warmth, gentleness, understanding, modesty, and strength. We will cry and may become the weakest link in the beginning, but the end makes us strong and rewarding.

I started going out to get back to normalcy. My sister once told me that when you go out, even if it's to pump gas, always look your best. I took her advice. I would wear a little makeup when going out and even got my hair cut and dyed. Yes, I was coming back to life until one day on the subway. I thought my heart had jumped out of my skin and onto the Metro platform. My ex was in the same Metro car. As we rode up the escalator at Potomac Avenue, we had a positive conversation. That's when I noticed firsthand and could visually tell his pain. Thereafter, we gradually became friends again. He expressed deeply that he loved and cared for me and that even though his timing inflicted lots of pain and suffering that it was never another woman involved, which was proven. We became good friends again, with jokes and laughter. Who in the hell does that? Mature adults. Forgiving adults. Dogmatically empathic friends.

Soon after, my blessings poured down on me. I began my new career with the fire department and became a first-time solo homeowner. The sky was cloudy, but through it all, it cleared up enough to allow the rays of the rainbow. **I had found my voice.**

CHAPTER 14

Another Health Scare: Defied but Relied On My Faith

Finally, I was living my life. I was content and happy. After all that I experienced at a young age, it was life lessons and testing my faith. The dating scene was open, and I welcomed it back. Stella got her groove back and some. The thought of getting married again was back on my plate, but only for the future, as I had found my voice again. During my pre-adolescent years and early adulthood, I experienced a normal healthy female regime: the joys and pains of cycles, the growth hormones, the temperaments of the highs and lows of estrogen, and its effects. The normal methodical anatomy of being a female. Until this happened...

A routine gynecology visit was a normal yearly routine for me. However, I kept having abnormal pap smears. I also started having mild symptoms of pain in the groin area when that time of the month came around. The results on that day of testing explained that I have polycystic ovarian disease (POC) and cannot get pregnant. POC is a hormonal dysfunction that causes small cysts to form on the outer edges of the ovaries, stemming from irregular cycles, and excessive hair growth, a definite reproductive imbalance that fails to regulate the eggs for pregnancy. Well, it affected both my ovaries. *Why me again?* I prayed every day and tried to reflect my Christianity through my actions, but this? What did I do to deserve this devastating news? How much more could I have handled? I was too young for this.

Did I do something horrible in my past that had come back to hunt or hurt me? However, this is a normal reaction that anyone would go through, but it depends on your stratagem's reactions to pro-actions to actions. I only told my close girlfriends and my family. It is unknown if this is hereditary. At least I don't think it is, so why did it choose me?

My options were not desirable. I felt that I was too young to adopt, and I did not want to go on any hormonal treatments. That was when I had a talk with God and expressed what I wanted and how to go about it. I changed my negative thinking to positive. I changed my diet and changed to healthier foods. I gave it all to God.

Well, after years of letting go and finding peace within myself, I became pregnant. I delivered a healthy, bald head baby girl, and hell, had two more healthy daughters thereafter.

CHAPTER 15

Fire and Desire: Such a Career

"When I am called to duty, God, wherever the flames may rage, give me the strength to save lives. Whatever it be age; I want to fill my calling and give it the best of me. Preserving life and protecting property."

—Fireman's Prayer

On February 13, 1989, I officially became a female firefighter/EMT. Looking back at it all. I stood in a long line with two male cousins to take the entrance examination in Northwest. I only did it just to see if I could pass it with no intention of becoming one. I had no desire because I was too dainty. Well, what do you know, I passed the exam? Talk about being shocked. With the lapse in acceptance to join officially, one cousin went into the government while the other joined the police force. I was working for my two medical internists. The fire department kept me on the list because I checked the box labeled not ready but kept me registered. Besides, I had passed the informative steps of the written exam and passed the physical agility along with the firemen's drag (with the heavy mannequin). My last step was passing the polygraph test with the Fairfax County Fire & Rescue Department, Fairfax Virginia. However, However, the District of Columbia Fire & EMS Department was more appealing for me. Therefore, I said bye Felecia. Then that final certified letter came, saying I was to accept the job, or they would take me off the list. So, after an intense conversation with my parents, I accepted the offer. A few of my girlfriends were not happy at all. My head physician boss had offered me more money to stay because I was an exceptional medical assistant. My extended family, however, was ecstatic, including my parents, especially my dad and his brother, and aunts on both sides of my tree. Here I come—DC Fire Training Academy.

I want to acknowledge and express my renowned honor and utmost respect to the female firefighters that paved the way before me, as I hope I have contributed to paving the way for future females coming abroad.

I developed and embraced a unified, everlasting bond with my brothers and sisters in the fire department. All fire departments exemplify a unique, unimaginable, perilous job that goes beyond recognition. Lay persons learn to have an exit plan (E.D.I.T.H) exit drill in the home and run out of the burning structure while trained firefighters run in and extinguish to save life and property.

So, what is fire? How hot can it get? Why do they mimic military operations? Can they see when extinguishing the fire?

Do firefighters get scared? When can I use a fire extinguisher? Let's begin with my definition of fire. Yes, that red flame or red glow is extremely dangerous and unbearably hot. Fire is a chemical change reaction that occurs between a combustible material—any material/liquid that breaks down and burns—along with oxygen, which results in the release of light, heat, flames, and smoke. It is a rapid oxidation process that can intensify, depending on the type of material/fuel that is burning. The temperature can range from 400 to 2,500+ degrees Fahrenheit. That is why firefighting gear, which is also called turnout gear, comprises a coarse, nonflammable, fire-resistive Kevlar, Nomex material. The entire PPE (Protective, Personal Equipment) can weigh forty-five pounds or more, depending on if they are carrying more equipment. Even the helmet/shield has its duty of protection against the heightened heat. It goes hand in hand with wearing the face piece/mask. The mask has a regulator that allows the hookup to the Self-Contained Breathing Apparatus (SCBA) to breathe in the fresh air and not the burning, contaminated fuel. The turnout coat has fire-protective material that has three layers: the outer shell, moisture barrier, and thermal lining. Also, it has wrist guards to help protect the wrist, and any skin exposed before putting on the gloves. It has reflective safety strips for visibility, along with several pockets to carry small equipment.

The turnout pants have reinforced materials on the knee to help when crawling to prevent injury and burns. The boots should be leather with a steel toe. The gloves comprise a protective ensemble. With all that, it's no wonder why small kids get scared of all these get-ups. Fire prevention is taught in a way that's easy to understand for each age group, so they don't get scared.

Can firefighters see when they are extinguishing a fire? Yes, and no, but more no. Some factors include the intensity of the fire and its location. Small, contained fires have visibility such as a small trash can fire. If a structure is in flames or and/or fully involved, there's no visibility. Here is when the training skills take place, crawling low, keeping your gloved hands on that hose, and feeling the floor for holes. When it's an orange or red glow, they are close to the fire or room involved. Once the fire is extinguished, you can see everything. Some fires are small and confined to one room, so they can see their way.

The alarm triggers a rush of adrenaline in firefighters because they never know how intense the fire is, how long it's been burning, if anyone's trapped, or if they can put it out. So yes, internally it is quite scary, but externally, because of the intensive training, they know what to do.

Fire departments execute the inclusive order of control like the military: an echelon of commanders. There are special operation procedures and guidelines in place, therefore paramilitary. All fire departments use military times just as well. Heck, I had to get used to military times. As a rookie, plenty of times I had to count—okay, well after 1200 noon add, so 0100 pm is 1300 hours, 0200pm is 1400 hours, and 0300 pm is 1500 hours, and so on.

Remember that fire has those components: fuel, oxygen, and the heat source: the good old Fire Tetrahedron. A fire extinguisher is used to break up that chemical change reaction that takes place at the base of the fire. Therefore, aim the hose at the base of the fire. P>A>S>S: pull the pin, aim the hose at the base of the small fire, squeeze the handle, and finally sweep the hose at the base, hoping to extinguish it. However, it is important to know that it is *only* and *only* used on very small fires such as trash cans, etc. Your back should always be positioned at the exit of the room so you can escape if it gets out of hand. New construction and residential homes include interior sprinklers. Government buildings have both sprinklers and fire extinguishers mounted. However, staff should still learn how to use the extinguisher and its location—hint, hint. Older brick and mortar do not have sprinkler systems and have fire extinguishers along with older homes (ABC universal one).

My dad always had that *damn* fire scanner on. Only if he had gotten hired back then, I know he would have been made chief. My dad was very knowledgeable of the fire jargon, fire pump equations, and definitely the radio frequency and its channels. I could have cared less. I had no interest in the fire service, so sometimes that scanner got on my nerves. He would turn it on as soon as he went downstairs in the morning until he went upstairs at night for bed. My mother had the nerve to keep buying him new ones. Really?

Preparation involved skills, training, intense exercises—jogging through the adjacent neighborhood, basic medical training, propelling and evolutions, various sizes and proper placement of ladders, and most importantly a positive attitude with determination. This was all taught at the fire training academy. This was where the *yes, sir* or *no, ma'am* standing to the side while saluting the white shirts came into effect. Oh, and they teach about a paramilitary regime, too. I met a few other women (even though men outweighed them in total) at the training academy, as most of us made it.

Our probation class was substantially large and, therefore, had to be divided. Some remained at the training academy for the allowable months for training. Others who did the two weeks—called the "ten-day wonders"—went directly to their assigned engine or truck company. I was a ten-day wonder. So here goes my story.

My assigned station was known as "Hogs on the Hill" because of its proximity to the once-historical Robert F. Kennedy Stadium, where the Redskins had their home games. An engine apparatus, a pumper (or the water truck which has been extinct) a battalion chief and his/her aide, two ambulances, and one medic unit were stationed there as well. The shift was twenty-four hours with two days off and a Kelly day, which you could work it for overtime or use it for a day off. I used my Kelly day as an off day for a long time. Being fit for my official uniform and bunker gear, I had my first shift work assignment to platoon #3.

My first barrier of disparity was gender-based, being a woman, and an Afro-American, let alone a petite little cute thang.

Before my assignment, I used to volunteer to train at the fire station near Eastern Market, thanks to my mother, who used to converse with the guys stationed there. Blockbuster was next door, so this gave her the notion of talking with the firefighters when they were out front. She informed them I had joined the department as a newbie. So, the officer allowed me to come to the two-story firehouse housed with a fire pole for practice. There, I met some guys stationed there that later became my family. This was where I first wore the heavy fire coat. Well, this day, it was the same routine of putting on the fire coat and running up and down the stairs from the second floor (where the sleeping quarters were located). As I ran to the top of the stairs, a fire brother, an Afro-American brother, stood at the top of the stairs with his arms folded. *Okay, what's this about?* I wondered. Out of his mouth, he snickered and stated, "I hope you are trying out to become an EMT because you ain't gonna make it as a firefighter," and then walked past me down the flight of stairs. WOW! This startled me and angered me. You're supposed to back me up, not put me down, proving that they did not want women on the job or specifically assigned to their circle (box alarm district). They only saw female firefighters as weak, apologetic, and pathetic, so they thought. After I regained my composure, I ran back down the stairs and later said, "See y'all next week," not knowing this was a true calling of discovering my voice in this predominantly male environment. YOU GO GIRL.

CHAPTER 16

My First Tour of Duty

My station was a one-level firehouse w ith t he fire apparatus's two ambulances and one medic unit parked inside the bay. The firehouse had a good-sized rear parking lot and a great repertoire with the neighbors. The bunk room was a good-sized unisex room next to the parked firetrucks. Wait. Hold up. Wait a minute. Do I not have my own room? Nope, I was told to select my bunk in the general population as we called GP. So, of course, I selected an empty bunk near the woman's bathroom. What did I get myself into? In line up, I was introduced to my coworkers, and it felt like they accepted me. I had a wagon driver, a pumper driver, and three backstep coworkers. Since I would be the rookie and probationer for a couple of months until I completed and passed the process, one of the firefighters had to be detailed out each time my shift worked. Later that morning, the chief and aide appeared and introduced themselves, but they had news for me, which turned out to be the best news. He said they had ordered me the wrong face mask. The size was a medium and I should have had a small. Therefore, I was commanded (remember, military) to be removed from duty and returned on my next scheduled tour or when my correct facepiece comes in. Yay! So, I got in my white Mitsubishi and took my happy self-back home—I still lived with my parents.

Welcome to my official tour of duty with my proper PPE. I had put my bedding, extra uniforms, bathing accessories, and all in my locker inside the woman's bathroom. After lineup and breakfast, I was introduced to my duties as the rookie—helping clean up the kitchen after each meal; my sole duty of cleaning the bunkroom side of the firehouse and helping where needed. I did not mind helping in the kitchen and making coffee, but I received a culture shock. I had to clean both the men's and women's bathrooms because it was on my side of the apparatus floor that entailed my cleanup duties. Hell, I didn't clean the toilets or mop at home. My dad did that chore. Say what? Oh well, I knew what I was getting into, so with a double-gloved hand, I cleaned and mopped. They taught me how to cut grass.

Mainly, I had to stay at the front desk to answer the phone and study because that's the duty of the rookie. This was when fire call boxes were on corners, and they had numbers on them. Those numbers were very important to firefighters, especially for the wagon drivers because it provides directions on how to get there—that was another requirement: having a valid driver's license because you will be groomed to eventually drive. This fire call box number gave you the hundred blocks, a guide to the address in need of fire or medical. Therefore, I had to learn our box alarm district by heart. So, file cards became my best friend. Later that morning, one of my coworkers told me it was a good thing I did not work that previous tour because of the wrong face mask. He said they had a house fire in which a baby had perished. Oh yes, indeed, I was happy I was not there. I don't think I would have been prepared for that and probably would have quit. My guardian angel had protected me until I received the proper equipment and training, not knowing more fires were on the horizon for me.

As the day progressed, after eating lunch and dinner, it was quiet. For all probationers, as well as me, we can relieve the watch desk (front desk) and do whatever except go to bed until 2000 hours—okay 0800 p.m. Luckily, we did not move a wheel that night. At 0600 a.m., I hauled out of there, especially since my relief (another probationer) came in early.

Man, oh man, my bedroom at home with blackened, thick curtains and feminine aromas never looked and smelled so good. After a bath and breakfast, I slept almost the entire day as my body was still trying to adjust to the twenty-four-hour shift—0700 a.m. to 0700 a.m. the next day. Again, what had I gotten myself into?

Even though my dad was not a Catholic like my mom and siblings, he had lots of Catholic pamphlets, a Holy Novena book, a Rosary, and a Scapula. A Scapula is a derivative of a Latin word for a symbolic sign of love, dedication, and strength. Monks wore the Scapula as a protective shield, especially when they had to conduct hard labor. It is not symbolized as a good luck charm, but a sign of salvation for protection and to live a life of heroic stature. After hearing about that poor angel that perished in that fire, I knew I needed more personal protection. So, I took my father's Catholic Scapula and wore it on every tour of duty inside my uniform pants pocket. I wore it until it faded and eventually tore—sometimes it ended up in the wash, accidentally, of course. It got to where I would panic if I did not wear it. Some may label it as fictitious, superstitious, idolization, or just downright Catholic Christianity. However, it became a part of my fire uniform throughout my years.

CHAPTER 17

Getting to Know My Place

A djusting to my new norm of being a ten-day wonder firefighter was acceptable, as I welcomed the soon-to-be profound profession. The engine company was becoming my steppingstone for maturity, self-preservation, and independence.

My shift continuously drilled and quizzed me. FYI: An engine, which was the Hahn model back then, was an apparatus that carried all the cross-lay hoses, ranging in various sizes, a standpipe rack on top, and a garden hose in the front. It also housed a five-hundred-gallon water tank as a reservoir until hooked up to the hydrant. The four members were: the wagon driver technician who knew pump operations, the OIC (Officer in Charge) who relayed the communication procedures while accompanying the line person, and the layout person who jumped off the apparatus at the hydrant and hooked up the line to it. The line person jumps off the piece, fully clothed in PPE, grabbed the crossline of the hose, and proceeded to the structure to extinguish the fire. At the same time, the wagon driver applied the specific PSI (pounds per square inch) of water that travels right into the hose. That pressure was no joke. My assignment was the line person since I was the rookie of the crew.

One day, we had a detailed officer in charge for that day. Yes, a break? Oh no, we drilled all morning. The drill consisted of me geared up, grabbing the cross-lay hose, then running through the firehouse to the rear of the parking lot, and with a charged hose, opening the nozzle and acting like I was putting out the imaginary fire. (That was a good time to have your car washed). The rest of the shift was quiet, thank goodness. I could not wait for my twenty-four-hour shift to end. Again, my bedroom was my heavenly sanctuary until my next tour of duty.

Back at work, everything was copacetic until this mid-morning.

CHAPTER 18

Box Alarm Number One

The routine regime: eating breakfast, cleaning the firehouse, and going back to the watch desk to study. Sundays were a bit of leniency for me, and other rookies, at least I thought it would be.

This Sunday was a sunny, beautiful day. All was quiet until the tone from communications, which was heard throughout the entire firehouse, came across as a box alarm for a house fire. FYI: a box alarm notifies and expels the four nearest fire stations: two trucks, a rescue squad, the chief and his/her aide, ambulances or medic, and any other special aide needed. Holy you-know-what! As I hit the button on the box at the watch desk to turn out the company, it also acknowledged communication that we fully received the assignment. Everyone ran to their specific duty on the firetruck. Boy, you better not have been in the bathroom or shower because you would have been short. As trained, I ran to my position as the line person and jumped into my running gear pants (which each firefighter does). I put on the rest of my gear while standing on my side of the apparatus while my wagon driver was haul-tailing with caution, of course, to the house fire. Boy, could he handle that wagon; we got there before the next closest due fire truck appeared. Remembering my drill from the previous shift, I was ready. After jumping off the rig, and pulling and flaking the hose, I proceeded to the front porch. The other companies were there and the truck company placed ladders up, etc. My layout person was with me on the porch as we donned our SCBA (self-contained breathing apparatus) and gave the thumbs up that we were ready to proceed inside. What happened to the sunlight? Darkness fell upon us quickly inside, as we could not see a thing. Our training taught us to follow the hose and not let go because that was our lifeline or ticket out if we got turned around. Guess what? We crawled right into a closet but immediately and safely got out of the closet and crawled down the hall. Whoosah…the orange glow and the crackling of the fire. Yes, it was extremely hot, but our adrenalin blanked all that out. The rescue squad was inside as well, checking the rooms for any victims. Thank God there was no one home. The crackling and heat became more intense as I knew we were close to the room that was fully involved. My training and my guardian angel kicked in as I opened the nozzle slowly to not get a water hammer and the pressure didn't throw my little self around like a kite. With my laymen holding my back, I quickly extinguished the fire. It became crowded inside as the other companies were doing their job. Then, suddenly, there came light. It was amazing that an interior fire can make it look like it was midnight at any time of the day. As I proceeded out of the house and stood on the porch, serious thoughts ran through my mind. Again, I was supposed to be at church with my sisters, wearing my best clothes and blazer—I was into blazers big time—or hanging out with my girlfriends or doing something girly. I just put out my first fire. The stench of the fire was on me, I was drenched in sweat, and hell -my hairdo was gone. Tears were about to run down my face. Quitting was heavy on my mind as I proceeded off the porch to go to my apparatus to get a drink of water and take off my gear. All fire apparatuses carry a large picnic size container of ice-cold water and cups. While doing so, other firefighters approached me, hitting my helmet like I needed a headache or had played my first football game, giving me kudos. A "job well done" or "congratulations" or "way to go, rook" from firefighters on the scene that I had never seen before. That's when it dawned on me—I received their welcome into the boys' club. This petite, muscle-toned female rookie had just extinguished her first structure fire, and that carried weight throughout the years to come. My first earned respect had surfaced. Back at the firehouse, the phone was ringing off the hook with congratulations. The most memorable call was from my two uncles: one a chief and the other a driver technician from another firehouse. They called to make sure I donned my fire gear properly, etc.

That was the highlight of my day. I will never forget it. Of course, my dad had his fire scanner on and heard the entire fire communication. I called him next, as he and my mother were extremely proud. So, the thought of quitting diminished as fire suppression remained with me for another five years. Even despite taking long baths (after my tour of duty ended) and deeply scrubbing to remove the soot embedded in the grooves of my fingers and constantly blowing my nose to remove the soot as well.

Was my voice becoming recognized as my guardian angels, once again, by my side?

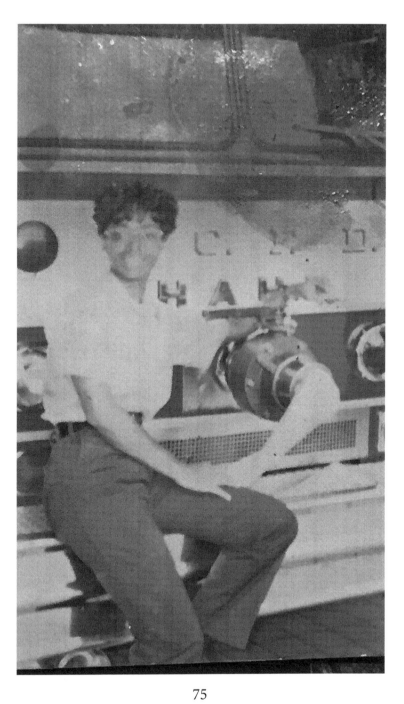

CHAPTER 19

To Be Young, Gifted, and a Black Woman

My First Racial-Gender Encounter and Some

A s the tours went on with the same routines, everything was coming along, and knowing the other coworkers (firefighters and EMS staff) made it more acceptable. My newfound position was becoming comfortable except for one position, another factor that the average layperson does not know. Anytime a fire engine, truck or squad backs into the firehouse from the street side, each fireperson has a certain position to stand (on the street) when getting off to hold traffic back. Well, still being a rookie in learning, there was one flaw. I just could not get it right. I kept getting off and going to the wrong position to stop traffic. I had no clue that my wrong sense of traffic direction was irritating my coworker. Well, I soon found out in the most unwanted, unpleasant way. Traveling back to the firehouse and stopping the traffic, it happened again. This time, though, he blurted out loud, "You stupid bitch!" Shocked, flabbergasted, hurt—it all turned into anger, and the old Southeast attitude came out. I followed him into the firehouse and loudly asked, "Who the hell are you calling a bitch?" My other coworkers rushed inside to gain control because I was losing it. Little me got right up in his face with my fist about to ball up, ferociously yelling, "I will be the last B you call." I think back to my maternal grandfather, who used to always say to me, "You always have that little fist balled up." That's when someone pulled me away just in the nick of time because I probably would have gotten fired. Why couldn't he have been sympathetic to my honest mistakes, as I was still a rookie? My wagon and pumper driver had a long talk with him. Later, he asked to speak with me to apologize. He admitted that his frustrations weren't really directed at me. Marital problems are a *bitch*, and he had some serious matrimonial indifferences: infidelity big time that was eating him alive and me being a female did not help. Dismayingly, I was his verbal outlet. Once I clearly understood his position and felt sorry for him, we slowly built a bond. We squashed the entire incident, but I'll never forget it.

Being a female in a predominately male career has its challenges, whether it's serious or all in fun, but the key is how you handle it—with a smile, tact, and respect.

Another incident occurred where someone put baby powder on my bed as a joke. Hell no, it was not funny. First, I could have submitted it as a discriminatory incident. Second, not on my pillow with my dry scalp. I nipped this in the bud immediately and stood my ground. After informing my officer, and with a tactful but boisterous voice, I dealt with it, and I went to bed with a smile. This was where I learned that firehouse games were common, but not with me, especially if they interfered with my integrity.

Being in this new world of male hormones, people approached me in dignified and undignified ways. Being a rookie and a woman, they were coming at me left and right. One firefighter had really harassed me to date him to where my pumper driver had to step up to him. My being labeled as "fresh meat" was never said again as my pumper driver became my firehouse dad and they knew he didn't play that game. End of story.

I found my voice for my personification even though it felt giddy to know I had choices to date, but I remained true to the game. True to my game. Its call:

R E S P E C T!

CHAPTER 20

The Test of Time
Box Alarm Number Two

Months had passed of being the firehouse rookie on my shift. This morning was different. They said we were getting a detailed officer that was from the old school. First, he was Caucasian. Second, he did not think women should be on the job. Third, I was told he was racist and for me to stay out of his way. So, when this officer, who was supposed to be in charge, assumed duty, I immediately picked up on his vibe. Being myself, I graciously said, "Good morning, sir," (again that military language) as we passed each other on the apparatus floor. Oh, snap! He did not acknowledge me at all, let alone look at me. They were not lying about him. So, I stayed at the watch desk to study and exemplify my normal firehouse rookie routines, hoping it stayed quiet until the shift ended and that I do not have to interact with this officer. Then the fire alarm sounded. It was for a house fire that was fully engulfed in flames and my company was the first due company to get there. I hit the acknowledgment button and turned out the company while running to jump in my running pants and jump inside the firetruck to finish putting on the rest of my gear. While my driver cautiously but swiftly got us to the scene, I did my same routine of grabbing the cross lay of hose, flaking it out as I ran to the front porch (with hose across my right shoulder- surprised I don't have shoulder issues), securing my gloves, and hair tucked inside the Nomex hood before putting on my helmet. This time, the detailed officer was there with me on the porch. He asked me if I was ready. I looked at him as if to say "Hell yeah, duh" with a neck roll, but instead, I politely nodded.

We donned the SCBA to breathe the positive pressured air into our face mask and advanced inside the burning inferno. As we proceeded to the area of origin—that heat, that glow, the crackling—I opened the nozzle as trained (30, 60, or 90-degree angle) and extinguished the fire. The other companies were also inside, maintaining their due positions. Being sweaty, my hairdo gone with the wind or fire, and adrenaline slowly coming back to normalcy, I proceeded out of the extinguished structure to the front porch. This time, it was different. As I was loosening up my belts to remove my SCBA from my back, I felt someone helping me take off my Scotts air cylinder. It was the *detailed officer.* He then shouted to others back at the apparatus to get me some water to drink, which we always carried that picnic-size container filled with ice water and plastic cups. Wow, see that? Experience that?

You feel it? I just proved myself to him. Excuse me, sir, but I was just doing the damn job that I was taught. Racial-gender stereotyping went out the window. Later that day, I became his fire buff and the talk of his conversation with other firemen who again were calling the firehouse congratulating our triumphant. From here on out, we had dialogues, not long, drawn-out ones but a decent hi or a nod.

Another significant fire incident that sticks out in my memory took place in the heart of Southeast. The area was mainly vacant, with a few subsidized apartments left. It was near the borderline of DC and Maryland. The firehouse alarm sounded for the Box Alarm at that location in Southeast. Upon arrival, along with the other dispatched companies, heavy smoke and fire were showing. It appeared to be in the basement of this small unit. Again, being the line person with the attack hose, we ascended to the area. However, we were confronted with a huge dilemma. The entrance was a tiny, narrow window that would test the guy's body-weight ratio, so I took the lead with permission from my officer. Soon as we arrived at that window, I removed my SCBA off my back and wiggled my way through the window. Once I landed on my feet, my air bottle was lowered down to me. I remember the squad was setting up for breaching (I think there were bars on the property), but my focus was extinguishing the fire. Therefore, I proceeded to the area of origin after putting on and donning my SCBA, I opened the nozzle on the fire, extinguishing it. As I proceeded outside to remove my gear after the wall was breached for egress, others were approaching me, saying, "Good job." Others were saying my officer got chewed out by the battalion chief in command. I immediately thought I had done something wrong. I extinguished the fire. I had all my PPE. What did I do?

Well, my officer approached me and apologized to me. His body language displayed it. I learned he had gotten chewed out for allowing me to enter through that window by myself for a few minutes alone and because of the dimension of the area, the fire could have flashed over, burning me to a crisp. Oh no, after hearing that, I even felt sorry for my officer for getting cursed out. But again, I gave praises to my guardian angel (again, who was my stillborn sibling), my faith, and, of course, my scapula that was in my uniformed blue pants pocket for preserving my me: my life.

Months passed, and I was in rotation, meaning stationed at other firehouses (in my battalion) for my twenty-four-hour shift. Some firehouses had some serious issues that I did not experience at my station. Some blacks refused to eat with the whites or have any dialogues. They conjugated within their same race. Some of my brothers did not even want me to even say a measly hi or eat with the other race. Being me, I paid no attention, but kept my eyes open as well. I articulated my authentic self, and I allowed no one to change me. But when the alarm sounded, they came together and did their job, but that was it.

Then there was the fireboat. Sometimes my rotation was detailed there. When not on a water call, we would sit out on the apron looking out into the Potomac River. The only thing I despised was the freaking spiders. However, I had to sharpen up my rope knots/tying skills, especially for docking the boats. I even had the pleasure of responding on the John Glenn Jr. fireboat (named after the astronaut). I had the experience of responding to boats in distress as well as medical calls on their boat or the pier. Being on the fireboat was a little less stressful because of the small number of dispatch calls.

I recall one incident during a night in the fireboat quarters. I had retired to the sleeping quarters, as I must have been exhausted because I did not hear the call. The crew had turned on the lights and that woke me up. I missed a fireboat run. Scared to death of being put on charges, they said the officer in charge told them not to wake me up. It was a high tide, and the winds were howling. The officer jokingly said they would have had to tie me up like a kite so I wouldn't blow away. Bammas. It was a medical call, anyway. Whoa, a sigh of relief. Sometimes when the fireboat was out on the water, the engineer tried to teach me how to steer the boat. The buoys, the readings of the tides and their importance, and again the knots. Heck, the only knots I knew were the knotless braids knots. Nevertheless, great education and experience.

On the other hand, they still all looked after me, regardless. In the firehouses, we joked respectfully, as my mouth was on point with them as well. I ate and conversed with whomever I desired. They taught me how to box using boxing gloves, lift weights, and bench press. The guys even shaped up the back of my neck with their clippers to keep my short hairdo looking fresh. Or as they would say, keep that kitchen looking tight. Within the different fire stations, they gave me their nicknames: Ruff Ruth, Dirty Ruth, Raggedy Ruth, Fire Eater, Firefighter Redmond, Baby Ruth, Ruthie Joe, Old Bird, Grandma and even Mama Ruth. I gained recognition and respect and achieved my solid foundation as a female firefighter, displaying my courage, perseverance, and character in establishing my boundaries. The audacity to help change their mindset—and I DID!

Throughout this storm, they heard my voice.

CHAPTER 21

Beautiful Bold and Blessed

D ays, months, and years had come and gone. The fire and EMS calls became the norm for me—back-to-back house fires. I recall extinguishing back-to-back structure fires that wore me out. Boy, I do not miss that at all nor being on watch at night to hear the alarm sound so I could turn out the company. This was my routine until…

One night, the alarm sounded for several vacant row homes on fire located in Ivy City, Northeast. Okay, I could handle this, at least I thought I could. It was exactly what the dispatcher had put out. Several fires were going on. Still being the line person, our crew extinguished one brick and mortar and was proceeding to the next. However, my crew jumped over the fence. No problem. I would hop over, too. Not! What in the world? I had to get help to hop over the fence. I was so drained that crawling inside the vacant property to put the fire out was excruciating. One thing I can honestly brag about is that I had never given my hose line up to another firefighter.

Well, there is a first time for everything. I had to give it to my layout person: lack to the point of no energy. What was wrong with me? Even my officer noticed my lack of drive. Hum!!! My coworkers on my shift started noticing my increase in appetite, which was ignored and quashed by me. However, one female paramedic stationed at my firehouse said, "Ruth, you are pregnant."

"Yeah, right, by whom? Whatever, you're tripping, girlfriend." I put that notion to rest quickly.

Oh, snap, she was right.

Before my pregnancy confirmation, the battalion chief's aide had detailed me to the ambulance. I was mad as hell because it was not my rotation. I made the best of it, though, as I got to know my EMS brothers. We had fun as ambulance partners. But I kept having a dull, annoying pain on my right side. One of our night transports to the hospital really made the pain ache.

The next morning, I went out on sick and headed to that fun-loving antiquated fire and police clinic that was located by the fire and police training academy. Oh, my God, that old clinic was something else! Chairs lined all down the hall for us to sit as one waited for the physician to see you according to your last name, and those brown paper shoes they made us wear. Well, after my assigned doctor asked me a bunch of questions, he suggested a pregnancy test. I agreed with confidence because I knew that was not the case.

Days later, I received a phone call from the clinic front desk personnel to inform me that my test was positive and that the clinic had made my appointment to come back. In denial, I said, "Can you repeat that? You sure you meant to call me?" She transferred me to the nurse

She said, "Ruth, baby, you are pregnant."

I hung up the phone and started crying. I got scared. I was single, had just purchased my first townhouse, and I was drinking Alize wine that always had a place in my refrigerator, with Hennessy on the top shelf for anyone who came to visit. I couldn't be.

After true confirmation from my private physician, my battalion chief and shift officer placed me in light duty status after they learned about the pregnancy. They immediately removed me from the twenty-four-hour shift because one night, my shift was dispatched on a call and I jumped up to go. That was the last station shift I worked. Oh my God, I was so loved being pregnant.

I was detailed to the fire chief's office until my due date. One civilian secretary said, "Girl, you have more lunch dates than ever." She was right, and I loved every bit of the attention. I had that glow as my stomach grew as I ate with pleasure. Some pregnant women cannot stand the smell or eat certain foods, especially chitterlings. But we ate at a soul food diner on 14th Street, Northwest, and I tore them things up with no problem. My main cravings were iced tea, fountain sodas (for the carbonation), and subs with hot peppers. I was beautiful and bold enough to prepare for single motherhood.

Because of my newfound majestic transformation, I chose not to exhibit any hostility or resentment, especially toward my partner. God had instilled this beautiful creation in me. Therefore, I danced with a big belly and a loving smile. Seeing my first sonogram, I was like a kid at Christmas. I cried tears with an abundance of love and joy at hearing the heartbeat and seeing the formation of birth.

I had delivered my first healthy daughter, watching the birth and the afterbirth via a large stationary mirror I requested in positioned so I could see everything. Really? Who makes that kind of request? My mother and sister were in the delivery room with me and were just as excited. I joked with my mom, saying, "You are smiling and cheesing so hard, your false teeth gonna fall out." They both were too scared to cut the cord, so I did it myself. I was a bad sista. Giving birth was a splendid occasion. My fellow fire constituents celebrated as well. I received flowers and monetary gifts. My favorite officer and his wife bought my baby girl lots of clothes from Hecht's, which is now Macy's. One special momentum that meant a lot to me was when I visited my firehouse with my baby girl. In the main sitting room, on the blackboard in large writing, stated that I had a six-pound baby girl. I was beautiful, bold, and blessed to be a single mother. Later in life, I was blessed with two more beautiful, healthy daughters.

CHAPTER 22

Transitional Worth

Life was great, glorious, and grand. I had my own house, own car, a good financially paying job, and I worked hard because I was a bad broad. *INDEPENDENT!* As well as being a single mom.

In the firehouse, things slowed down for some odd reason. Fire calls became minimal. Seemed like all we did—run medical calls: gunshot victims, stabbings, other health-related calls—to the point it was monotonous. I felt doom and gloom like the party was over. The conversation with my dad changed my trajectory of firehouse depression and resignation. He distinctly said, "It's time for a change within."

With five years under my belt, I could apply for any technician position that was posted. I took his advice, applied, and became a certified fire inspector/certified pyrotechnician. Yes, no more firehouse shenanigans. A Monday through Friday (with overtime), eight-hour shift with a plethora of overtime. We wore white shirts and black uniform slacks.

Kind of felt somewhat important. I was proud to be a part of this elite group as I gained another fire department family. Training was intense but purposeful as we learned to do inspections and visually detect violations with fines if needed. Ward 6 was my section of the city. We had to inspect so many establishments a day and record them on the worksheet. Even though we drove our personal cars, at least the division gave us Fire Prevention Inspector Placards to avoid getting tickets. Sometimes we paired up or assisted another inspector with a major job, but mostly, I traveled solo in my ward.

This particular storefront inspection located on Pennsylvania Avenue, Southeast, was a psychic place. As I walked in and politely introduced myself, the owner rudely said, "Okay, so why are you here?"

What the…? Excuse me, miss thang. I just smiled and said, "Well, you're the psychic, so you should have an idea." Surprisingly, she laughed as that broke the ice.

After doing my thorough inspection of the place, she said, "Let me read your palm."

"Okay, go for it."

Wow! With honesty and truth, she asked if I had ever written something major. I said, "Nope."

"You will be publishing something or be published," she said. Of course, I did not believe one word she brewed out.

Fast-forward—Look at God! I had been published in a prestigious newsletter and I am writing this *memoir.*

All the fire inspectors were governed to maintain that quota for their specific ward inspections. I inspected my quota each day with no problems. Not knowing that I was amid building up my resume as the Fire Investigations Unit sparked my interest. I got permission from my lieutenant and approval from the fire marshal to become a ride-along one day a week for my eight-hour shift. Therefore, I kept my fire gear in my trunk. The Fire Investigation Division was on Georgia Avenue, Northwest. It was every Wednesday or Thursday that I traveled and signed in at FIU. Your girl was the first firewoman that started training there, not realizing I was becoming a trailblazer. Months later, another female fire inspector followed suit, with more women to follow years later. However, being trained by the well-qualified senior investigators was beyond words. I worked with each one and their partner, giving me the street knowledge of inspecting property/vehicle after the fire had been distinguished. This was intriguing to me as I embraced it all.

One particular afternoon, after picking up my lunch from the famous sub shop on 11th Street and Pennsylvania Avenue, Southeast (a G-man sub), I received a message on my pager to call one of the seasoned, veteran fire investigators. Yes, we had pagers.

He said, "Hey, you want to come with me to visually see a fire autopsy?"

Having a medical background with anatomy/physiology under my belt, my response was, "What time to meet?"

Being from the 7th Fire Battalion, we had to know all the parking lot numbers at Robert F. Kennedy Stadium, as well as all the building numbers at DC General Hospital. So, I knew where the DC morgue was located. To preserve my tasty sub, I stopped by my parents to place it in their fridge as I drove to meet the investigator. We met in the lobby at the morgue.

"Have any apprehensions?" he asked.

"Nope, just curious and a little nervous." Wrigley's double mint chewing gum became my friend that day, shoving two sticks in my mouth.

The technicians approached us to guide us to the actual autopsy room. Here we go!

Putting on the gown, gloves, and mask for me, we entered the embalming room with the unfortunate deceased fire victim on a metal bed that contained drainage. As I looked around my environment, there were tubes, machines, tools, weighing stations, and enormous, large sinks with draining vents all around. Then, the stench of formaldehyde. My tomboyish curiosity and pre-fire investigation status were ready as the mortician and other techs came into the room. I could have turned around and dodged left, but not me. Because of the nature and graphics, I will not deliver what and how a full-body autopsy is conducted. It's definitely not for the weak or layperson. The mortician knew I was in training and thoroughly explained her step-by-step examination and measures. Talk about chewing and wearing my gum out of its flavor. Whew, child. I learned what organs were to be weighed on that large scale, especially if the deceased was a donor. As the autopsy concluded, I did okay. In this fire, I did not realize this was preparing me for my own fire-related deaths as a fire investigator.

And by the way, the sub sandwich was thrown in the trash as well as the gum. It took several teeth-brushing sessions and copious amounts of mouthwash (gargling) to remove that taste of formaldehyde from my mouth.

CHAPTER 23

Preservation of
Life and Property

Doing routine inspections and riding along was becoming my normal routine. This one afternoon, my coworker and I had just finished a major inspection and were about to get lunch—I had to get my eat on—until I got a page to return to the office ASAP. Somewhat nervous, we both tried to figure out the circumstance. Did one of those bamma clients complain about me? I didn't know.

We arrived at the office and the first thing the fire prevention chief asked was, "Where is your gear?"

"Sir, in my trunk."

"Okay, as of tomorrow, you are to report to the Fire Investigation Unit as your eight-hour shift until further notice."

Talk about shocked, ecstatic, and on cloud nine. My partner was happy for me as well. (Months later, he became an investigator, too). Then the senior investigator walked into the front office and I was immediately assigned to him as his rookie. Having a full day per week with the senior investigators, my experience was growing. Even though the drive was a longer commute for me, getting there and going home to Upper Marlboro, Maryland. Throughout my days, I learned the real definition of origin/cause—how to conduct on-the-scene fire interviews along with on-the-scene fire photos. One day, they let me loose to write my own report (even though my mentor had written the original report). Boy, oh boy—the lieutenant had red ink all over my report (for corrections). *okay, I'm learning dude, so ease up*. But this taught me the proper technique and flow in typing a fire report because it's a legal document. And he never lied.

Everything was going smoothly, getting adjusted to my new pre-assignment until the office started getting complaints about me being detailed there. Really? So, the fire marshal made a list of interested fire inspectors to rotate going up to FIU (fire investigation unit). I was enraged, let down with heavy disappointment. They all knew about my detailed assignment, so why know? But what pissed me off the most was that my name wasn't even on the rotation list, not realizing the rationale behind it all. Sometimes we must stop, breathe, and get out of our own way. Then the next whammy was we all had to take the FIU written examination. I was too agitated to see the light at the end of the tunnel. Well, a few (along with myself) passed the exam. At the end of it all, some accepted their new position while others went back to their fire inspection post. Now the light had shone as I finally understood the logic of going through the proper channels and weeding out the not-so-serious ones. I had to make some different arrangements at home as well.

Passing and becoming a certified fire investigator was another steppingstone for my career. Taking several investigation courses helped solidify my newfound position.

FYI: A fire investigator goes inside the property after the firefighters have extinguished the fire and finished overhauling (meaning, pulling floors and ceilings to make sure of no hidden fires) therefore exposing all types of toxic materials that had burned.

I had reached over one hundred different fire calls to determine what, how, and when it started after the fire was extinguished as the requirement for becoming certified. I was proud of myself for determining the origin and cause—whether it was accidental, incendiary, or undetermined. One insurance adjuster gave me a generous compliment. It was a car fire and after thoroughly examining all causes, interviews, and photos, I determined it was accidental, and my report reflected how and where it started. He said my determination was right on point. For many more calls, I assisted or became the lead fire investigator.

A couple of years later, the unit had the pleasure of working with Alcohol, Tobacco and Firearms (ATF) as their investigators had to get a certain number of calls to keep up their certification. Being me, I grew a phenomenal rapport with them, to the point a few had asked me to join the ATF family. That was not on my radar as they traveled too much and I was not about to leave my family, especially when duty called outside the DMV (Washington, DC, Maryland, and Virginia area). They gave me some pointers on how to conduct fire origin/cause and proper PPE as well and vice versa.

On one hot afternoon, an apartment fire was dispatched along with FIU. My ATF partner (a different senior FIU veteran) and I arrived on the scene. The firefighters assigned to the box alarm quickly extinguished the fire. Because my partner was one of the first armed fire investigators, he had to arrest the person of interest who was still on the scene. This made me become the lead fire investigator. I did a thorough examination, interviews galore, and careful, detailed fire scene photos. Utilizing my learned skills and remembering the movie, *The Bone Collector*, I conducted the interior examination like in the movie—following the grid. Seriously. Examining from top to bottom, floor to ceiling, noted the building material of the unit that had contributed to the intense heat. I checked out all the appliances and the electrical panel while ATF did their assistance. I had detailed photos as well.

I mentioned earlier that fire reports are legal documents. A couple of years later, while I was on maternity leave, I got subpoenaed for court on this fire case. I'd just had my third daughter. Therefore, I called our fire union, and they stated it was a must. Long story short and without going into the detailed legal specifics, I met the attorney. This was my first rodeo, and I was shocked when I stepped into his office. Not only did they have a copy of my fire report, but they had enlarged every photo I'd taken to fit on 8.5-x-11-inch easels.

We thoroughly went over my report, depicting and explaining every photo. But the big kicker and nerve wrecker was being interviewed by the jurors to see if I could stand competent if selected. Well, I was the lead investigator that stood at this grand jury trial. My assessors, ATF, and the armed fire investigator stood trial. My thorough fire knowledge and skills led to a serious conviction. I had won my very first arson case. Days later, my FIU officer called me into his office and said he wanted to be the first to congratulate me as he handed me a certified letter from the Superior Court in DC on my job performance well done. I still have that letter.

In the fire, I found my voice.

I cannot recollect how many FIU calls I responded to thereafter, as well as fire-related death calls. My very first death-related call was determined accidental because of the individual smoking in bed. Again, I was the lead investigator making all the calls on this incident. Because it was death-related, the MPD (Metropolitan Police Department) was on the scene as well. They are the ones that declare the death on arrival. So, after they conducted their investigation and agreed on the cause, the scene was left for me and my partner. I took photos of the deceased, who was found dead, in the position found: kneeling beside the bed before they took the body to the morgue. Long story short, I had to go to the morgue to complete my fire report. Again, another visible autopsy. Again, the female mortician explained everything in detail. She then asked me, "Do you know how we determine if the victim was alive during the fire?" The lungs. They were blacker than midnight, meaning the victim inhaled all that smoke and soot. Years passed, and I had maybe two or three more death-related fire calls.

But this one call opened my eyes and changed my viewpoint. It was a residential fire that was fully involved in flames. The property was handed down to the occupant as a family heirloom. Even though I classified it as accidental, the occupant was so distraught and hurt. The occupant cried so hard, stating he lost everything that was left to him. This hurt me deeply. This was when I realized that back in the day, as a young fire rookie, experiencing that adrenaline of wanting a fire to put out was not the thing. It was about preserving *life and property*. This hit home for me, giving me a different perspective, as I had property of my own.

Another health obstacle: Having numerous fire investigation calls under my belt, everything was going well for me until this happened. During this investigation, I begin to experience a terrible sharp pain. It felt like a knot was forming in my groin area. My female partner said to go off sick as soon as we finish this call and return to the firehouse. Fast forward: one of my polycystic ovarian cysts had ruptured. So here I go again, having another female medical procedure done. *What the hell?*

CHAPTER 24

Glowworm Epithet

FIU had experienced some changes that did not resonate with me. It unconsciously affected my demeanor, coming home feeling frustrated and burnt out. Twofold: I loved being a female fire investigator technician, but I wanted out at the same time. Therefore, when the technician spot on the hazmat opened, your girl applied and got accepted. Another career change within my career.

Hazmat technicians were called "glowworm: because of the different PPE they wore, depending on the type of hazardous call (Level A, B, C, and D suits). I now belonged to another group of fire family as I became part of the elite Special Operations Division.

The Hazardous Material Units was housed inside a firehouse along with the fire apparatus/ambulances and chief. We had to cook for a lot of folks, so the hazmat unit was in rotation as well to cook breakfast or dinner. Sometimes, I hated cooking for these guys—take about picky eaters.

And again, back to sleeping in GP doing another twenty-four-hour shift. My shift was awesome, especially my crew. When not responding or coming from a call, we would put on our headphones and start singing or whatever made us happy. They seriously became my family (still to this day). Many hazmat calls were so long that I carried my personal mobile commissary. I filled my African print backpack with candy, in which my crew had to take turns buying the refills. Our favorite was the colorful Jolly Ranchers. I'm surprised we weren't called the toothless glowworms with all that consumption of sugar. On a serious note, it was not a joke. Being in special operations, we had to take lots of classes for certifications/recertifications. I finally got to travel. Intense classes like weapon of mass destruction classes, radiation classes, meter classes, trained to properly wear the appropriate gear classes (where pepper spray or some type of agent sprayed around our N95 to make sure we could not smell it), numerous classes to name. Yes, some serious stuff was not to be taken lightly, and I adhered.

The reason we stayed on a hazardous call for long periods of time is because of the specific/timely preparation for that specific call. Inside the unit, each person had a role: driver, officer, two entry individuals, and the research person. Each job had a detrimental part. The meters had to be logged on and ready to go; the research person had to be on that computer looking up the alleged or known chemical. This gave the information to park uphill or downwind, what type of gear to wear, what type of gloves, etc. Once we arrived on the scene, the assigned special op fire company had to help get the hazmat entry folks dressed. The entry team had to be properly taped and secured to avoid any possible leakage entering the suit. The boots had me flopping around like Flipper the Dolphin. And just like in firefighting, I would enter the area of origin with a decent hairdo but would come out looking like I'd been in a fight. That suit can get hot, especially if we are inside the scene conducting lots of metering and testing.

I remember when we had the anthrax scare. Sorry to say, but I was glad my shift was off because of the positive hits. However, we still ran up and down the streets because of the idiotic copycats. It was sad that individuals would do pranks for fun to them, but costly to us because we had to follow protocols as if it was another hazardous call.

Being in special operations, we had so many in-house training/drills. Water rescue drills on the big fireboat or on the low-fire water vessels, winter ice drills at Hain's Point, which I had to wear a wet suit (after securely being tethered in), take the ice spikes, and basically walk the water to the point of our designated rescue spot. This was one time I was glad to be lightweight because if that ice had broken, like the phrase goes- down goes Frazier. Seriously, the wet suit's purpose is to assist in floating as well as keep you dry. Then I would have been pulled back to shore by the tethered rope. So, I was not worried at all. I participated in high-angle drills to low-angle drills, meaning confined spaces. If a rat had come across my path, then they would just have had to put me on charges, for this Sista wasn't going to comply. Anyhow, I did extrications, whether it was vehicular to stuck elevators. You name it; I did it.

However, this one water rescue drill brought out my panic mode. The guys (as usual) helped me don and burp my wet suit. This was extremely important because it helped with floating. Well, it was my turn to climb down the dock stairs backward and then lay back and float in the Potomac River in Southwest. Okay, back floating was my thing until they said, "Everyone, raise up to float upwards," like bobbing until they get the drill started. I could not do it. A few of my coworkers came over to lean me up to float upright. That's when I panicked and told them to leave me alone and let me continue to float on my back. The anxiety hit me hard, realizing I was floating in that large body of water and looking straight up at the sky. The fireboat/station to my right and the Spirit of Washington cruise vessel to my left. No wonder I panicked. Floating next to that monstrous ship that I once partied on. That's one drill I was so happy they canceled. I floated back until I could reach the stairs to the dock with their help. That suit came off me quick and in a hurry.

Again, I gave praise to God and my guardian angel for protecting me (still wearing my catholic scapula in my uniform).

CHAPTER 25

Whirlwind of Emotions Circa 2015

Being a member of special operations was utterly rewarding, but here I go again. Tired of being in the firehouse, tired of the twenty-four-hour shift, tired of cooking for a large crew, tired of missing home, tired of being tired—where did my femininity go? This evoked a serious whirlwind of mixed emotions. Second-guessing yourself can be recklessly escalating. Therefore, it was time for a change again before time changed me.

Reflecting on my pinnacles of success allowed me to let go and let God. He said it was okay to breathe and step back, not knowing the real reason. So, the Fire Prevention Division knocked on my door until retirement.

Timeless travel for classes, recertifications, and all; I became a fully certified ICC (International Code Council) Fire Inspector for the DMV. My credentials became impeccable, putting a smile back on my face. Instead of returning as a ward inspector, I became a charter school inspector. Also, I had the most amazing details: concerts, the Washington Nationals opening games, and utilizing my pyrotechnical skills during the Fourth of July fireworks at the mall. The most monumental overtime was the presidential detail with President Barack Obama and his full-force security team. I remember the time President Obama got out of his secured buggy to walk instead. Boy, those guys were on it. I could see him walking into the grounds before entering the detail. I was detailed when his daughter graduated from high school, which was exciting as well. Another big moment for me was the detail of the live taping honoring Ms. Aretha Franklin. We all looked sharp in our dress blues and shiny black patent leather shoes. You couldn't tell me nothing, especially because your girl was stationed inside the taping, diligently doing my job, keeping the aisle clear, especially near the exit doors. I saw all the stars presenting awards and accolades about Ms. Franklin. Mariah Carey, Janelle Monae, Jennifer Hudson, and that fine Ice Cube, to name a few. Then the honoree approached the stage in the historic fashion of wearing her mink coat and carrying her purse.

Being a school inspector wasn't bad, especially with the great teamwork, despite occasional opposition of fire code violations. Getting the schools to comply with and abate their problems felt awesome/rewarding. A few schools almost had to face being shut down, but it worked out. But dealing with the school's fire drills and evacuation plans with their staff was not an easy job. It was tedious, precise, accurate, and had to be done in the specified timely order. Otherwise, it was all okay position.

One morning in the office, I had a lot of paperwork to copy. So, while walking to the Xerox machine, my right knee took a dip and gave out. My coworker witnessed the entire episode and came to my aid. As days went by, the knee started acting up again. Off to the fire department clinic to get an MRI and be placed on sick leave. I finally had a procedure done on the knee, followed by extensive therapy at Washington Rehab. (I forgot to mention that the injury to this knee originated from sliding down the firehouse pole when I was assigned to the Hazmat Unit. Someone had gotten it wet when washing their EMS unit, which caused the pole to become extremely slippery. Therefore, I had no grip. I eventually slammed down the apparatus on the floor, injuring the knee and later experienced a torn meniscus). My female therapist was very thorough, but nice. You know I made friends there joking, laughing, but getting the job done so I could get back to full duty, which was no joke and required evolutions with full gear with or without the SCBA tank on my back, being timed going up and down the stairs, treadmill, climbing up and down the ladder, firemen drag with the dummy and more.

During this timeframe, I had scheduled a complete physical with my primary physician (not the fire department doctors) because I noticed my weight change. I was ignoring my personal, physical, and emotional body changes. I went from a size 8 to a 6. It really hit me when my pants were sagging. Was I under that much stress? Finally, I stopped, looked, and listened. Pay attention to your body language or it will get your attention.

My physical went well, despite the weight loss (charted from my previous physicals)—EKG was normal, blood work, and urinalysis.

"You have not had a mammogram in over three years," my doctor said.

Despite her medical lecture, I made an appointment at Washington Radiology. Here we go again.

My 3D mammogram showed some questionable markings, so I had to go back for breast biopsies. No big deal, as I could handle this. Women have one or two breast biopsies taken all the time. Being prepped with their hospital gown and footies, they escorted me to the *exam room*. Oh, my God, I was a bundle of nerves. The breast biopsy table was a hard-ass, wood-feeling table. As I lay still, flat on my stomach, with my head turned, with no pillow, the physicians came into the exam room and explained the procedures—not procedure. My intuition told me something was not right. That hard table was raised high with the machines placed underneath with tools, needles, and specimen jars as my breast was positioned in the stationary hole in the table. A total of five needle core biopsies were taken from my breasts (three from the left and two on the right). Each tissue extracted was carefully placed in formalin-filled containers.

By the time it was over, tears were forming because the crook in my neck was horrendous. I had serious neck pain as they tried to massage it out. Meds were waiting for me when I got home, along with a hot shower. Whew.

Still on FD medical leave and going to therapy for that knee injury, everything was going to be okay. I was near finishing therapy to get back to full duty.

I will always remember this day in my life. I picked up my oldest daughter as we drove through Georgetown. At the light, my cell phone rang. It was the doctor's office, so I pulled over to talk. I heard but didn't hear. She asked if I could talk as she had my results, or if I wanted to wait until I got home. Okay, I knew pregnancy was out the window, so maybe my labs were abnormal. My response was, "It's good to talk." The blood work came back normal, including my iron level. So why was I losing weight? Then she said your biopsies came back POSITIVE for breast cancer. She instructed me to call the office first thing in the morning, and she apologized. God showed me the way and steered my car home safely from Northwest DC to Bowie, Maryland, as I was numb. My daughter did not know what had just happened. Desensitized and paralyzed, I continued with my motherly duties when we returned home. I cooked dinner even though my appetite had completely diminished. I helped my youngest daughter with homework, cleaned the kitchen, and made sure my daughters were in their rooms for bed. Mothers always tend to the family first. As women, we carry out various duties but constantly ignore ourselves. We are expected to exemplify strength and courage and be a nurturer, a matron, and sorceress, along with other positive attributes, only to lose our footage sometimes, causing a lack of self-reflection that can cause a plethora of health setbacks. And STRESS is a MF.

Showered to prepare for bed after my home was quiet and still, I closed my bedroom door, grabbed the house phone, and went inside my walk-in closet to call my mother. Still in disbelief, my oldest sister answered the phone, and I fell apart. She immediately put my mother on the phone. A mother's love is endless. The one phrase that still sticks in my head was her saying that "It's not a death sentence—breast cancer, that is. Technology has come a long way. So, try to calm down." After what seemed like a long conversation, I hung up only to call my close girlfriend from the Fire Prevention Division. We both cried as she respectfully tried to calm me down as well. Why me? The poignant, meaningful spoken words she bellowed out to me have never left my heart, even to this day.

I HAVE BREAST CANCER and I AM SCARED and FEEL ALONE.

CHAPTER 26

Being on the Frontline of Your Health

How did sleep knock on my door that night? My mind was in overdrive with emotion, guilt, and questions. As soon as the girls were off to school, I called my physician as instructed and she referred me to the oncologist at Sibley Hospital. Once I scheduled the oncology appointment, they advised me to bring an advocate with me, and thereafter, which is extremely important. So, my niece was my advocate.

What was so puzzling was the oncologist did another breast examination and felt NO lumps. I answered all medical questions, including my family's history. No one in my family had breast cancer, so why did it choose me? My contributory factors were stress, which is a normal natural chemical hormone that has a fight-or-flight syndrome and reacts differently from a positive to a negative state, which is when the body begins to compensate to that negative state; all that sugar intake as it feeds cancer cells (remember the number of sodas I had consumed, especially during my early years in the firehouse- drinking 4-5 sodas a day even with breakfast); my toxic environment—firefighting, inhaling the floating fumes from the released unknown chemicals—possibly the soot that was on my skin could have absorbed; and they claim hair dyes with lye can contribute as perms was a two to three-month regimen for me. I really lost my footing of being on the frontline of myself, my health, worth, and self-survivorship. What a wake-up call.

After the exam, my niece and I met in her office for a consultation. The oncologist explained in precise detail the results of the findings, and her professional scope of when, where, and what will happen before and after surgery. She had even drawn out an outline of the locations of the cancer tissues on each breast. Fast forward to another scheduled appointment to finalize surgery. Again, my niece accompanied me. When the oncologist discussed a few things from the first appointment, she said, "You look puzzled." Yes, I did, because I didn't believe she'd said what she'd said. My niece remembered every detail. See, it's so important to have that advocate, and I was grateful for her presence. I was there in body, but not in mind, and that was to be expected. The surgery was scheduled for May, but I begged to have it right after my youngest daughter graduated from elementary school. I was not about to miss that special occasion. Surgery would be at Sibley's Hospital Sullivan Breast Cancer Center in June 2015. My insurance was already approved for the left mastectomy and the right lumpectomy. Everything was arranged and confirmed. Papers were signed as they gave me a binder filled with breast surgery information: tabs for procedures for pre- and post-surgery, a tab for support programs, tabs for appointments or any other imaging testing, and one for "cancer-fighting food and spices." I was even introduced to the referred plastic surgeon that would be in the operating room as well. The medical plan was synchronized, solidified, and set in stone…except for me.

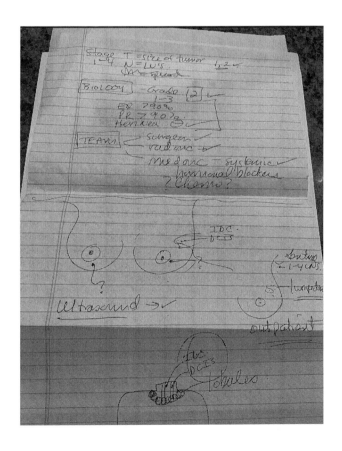

CHAPTER 27

Stage 1 Her2 Negative in Situ Breast Cancer

My Personal Understanding About Me

B reast cancer has no filter on gender, size of breast, or age range anymore. However, it can be hereditary, a genetic mutation. My finding was not hereditary. Its exposure to radiation and/or environmental factors such as smoking, or maybe secondhand smoke, can trigger its progression. Once the diagnosis is confirmed, it is determined what stage of the disease has formulated based on the progression, size, cancer cells in the lymph nodes, and location throughout the body. There are Stages 1 through 4, with Stage 0 being very minute and noninvasive and Stage 4 (de novo) being invasive and having metastasized. The TNM factor is also considered: the tumor, the node, and if it has metastasized.

Ductal Cancer in Situ (DCIS) develops in the milk ducts and has not spread to other breast tissue. Invasive Ductal

Carcinoma (IDC) also develops in the milk ducts but has spread outside the ducts as well.

Her2 positive or Her2 negative is also determined by the pathological finding of that specific protein that contains antibodies and attaches to that protein from the tissue biopsy taken from the patient. Here is where they can recognize the Her2 protein. If the results show a 0-1+ results, it means the cells have very little to none of that protein as the opposite for Her2 positive.

Being Stage 1 Her2 negative, the choice of treatment is tamoxifen for five to ten years, which is always changing based on oncology studies. However, if my level changes from any of the above factors, I would be a candidate for radiation or a specific amount of chemotherapy treatment.

Where is my Guardian Angel? Where is God when I seriously need Him?

CHAPTER 28

Faith vs. Faith

I cannot muster all the afflictions placed on me in April 2015. Even though the insurance company accepted the surgery, being diagnosed with this disease was unacceptable to me. My focus had to be to get back to full duty so I could build up enough leave for the upcoming breast cancer surgery.

The saying "Life goes on and so does time" is a metaphor that is very hard to decipher, but so true. I'm still a mother with girls and grands who need me. Hell, I need myself. So, I put that smile back on my face, wiped my tears, began thinking positively, and kept it moving.

To be placed back on full duty, one must pass the agility test. I could not wait to get this over with and move on to the next medical agenda. Here we go again.

Everyone was so in tune with the new television show Empire. We used to make sure dinner was served; the house was cleaned, and homework was done to tune into that show. The finale was coming on this Wednesday evening, so I wanted to run out to get dinner. Folks and arenas were having Empire parties. Chipotle and Chick-Fil-A were on the menu this night. My middle daughter was already home from college on spring break and was waiting for us to get home. I had to pick up my youngest daughter from middle school and then get to the Chick-Fil-A—I had already ordered Chipotle and dropped it off at home. Okay, my oldest and my two grands wanted to ride along, so they sat in the back. Cool. Everything was copacetic. The weather was perfect, and the traffic was light. After picking up my child from Ernest Just Middle School in Mitchellville, Maryland, we headed to the fast-food place. We came upon a four-way intersection with my traffic light facing east. Hell, I was not going any faster than the speed limit as the police sat at his light, going north. Once my light turned green, I proceeded slowly, then my youngest yelled, "She's coming at us!"

"Who is coming?"

She yelled much louder, "Ma, she is coming right at us on my side (front passenger side)."

Then I heard a loud boom. I am not sure if I blanked out, but I could hear my daughters crying hysterically. "Why can't my mom open her eyes? Mom, wake up!"

My airbag deployed, and the dust from it was in my eyes. I was trying to tell them that, but the words were not coming out. Trying to open my eyes from the deflated airbag powder, I eventually was able to open my eyes and look out my window. I couldn't even count how many cops were on

119

the scene and bystanders who saw the accident. My glasses had flown off my face and were on the floor. My cell phone had flown in the back seat from the center console. Thank you, God, for seatbelts because the grands were unharmed but shaken up. I can't recall how many badges of blue surrounded my car and directing to diverse the traffic.

Then one of the young, fine-looking cops said, "Damn, her car is total."

"How in the hell?" I muffled out my mouth.

He said, "Ma'am, somehow you maneuvered your Honda from hitting your daughters' side and went head-on with the other vehicle."

Being that frontline firefighter, fierce Glam-ma, I got out of my car and walked around my vehicle. That adrenaline had kicked in, but that was the worst thing to do—walk around after a serious motor vehicle accident. It was, for sure, a head-on collision. There I was, out of the car, surveying the damages until another cop instructed me to get back in my vehicle until the ambulance arrived. Suddenly, a sharp pain radiated from my finger up to my right elbow. All hell, I had a broken finger, displacement—self-diagnosing. There was a larger space between that finger than the normal gap.

As I kind of complained about my aching arm, my daughters were more distraught than me. I informed them to call their father to pick them up and get all my information out of the car before the tow truck came. The individual that caused the accident remained on the scene but was so upset herself from hurting me and totaling my favorite 2011 Honda Accord. It was dark brown with an awesome, booming radio system. Anyhow, she asked the cops to check on my girls and grands. Then my ride pulled up—the ambulance. Inside the unit, I called my oldest sister and told her what had happened and that I was being transported to the good old Prince George's Hospital. Next, I called my bestie from Fire Prevention to ask her to inform the lieutenant and/or chief about my accident. Then I mentioned how all the cops were there, and that they were too young for me to book (that old school jargon). We both laughed hysterically. I have never experienced being in Prince George's Hospital's emergency room, but it was the closest hospital.

After returning from getting x-rays, my oldest sister, who was on her way to an Empire party at the MGM Grand at the National Harbor, Maryland, arrived and waited with me until my discharge.

In the meantime, the mounted flatscreen was high on the wall and turned to Fox Channel 5, so we had our own Empire party. Everyone sitting in the ER waiting room had snacks and something to drink as we looked at the show. Surprisingly, it wasn't crowded; other folks were home watching Empire, where I wanted to be, but as I looked around at my surroundings, it kind of felt like home. They were shouting and laughing, and some were cursing about the famous Empire character Cookie. At the same time, my youngest daughter (who was in the car during the accident) kept calling my cell phone, thinking I wasn't coming home. I finally calmed her down and told her to go into her sister's room until I got home, and I would be home.

Finally, they called me to the back room and said, "You were right, a fifth metacarpal displacement, aka fissure injury, aka fractured." So, they put a splint on my finger, gave me some pain pills and a prescription, and sent me on my merry way. At least we looked at the entire one-hour season finale of Empire. FYI: please adhere to your vehicle's guidelines. It's there for your safety. If the airbag could break my finger, imagine what it would do to a child, which is not the age or weight to sit in the front passenger seat.

That night I was restless, trying to resonate with all this. *Why me?* I was trying so hard not to interrogate my faith, but it was becoming questionable. But I knew God still had my back: faith vs. faith.

The next morning consisted of body aches and raccoon eyes along with the aching finger. Indescribably confused, I worried about my job status. I knew the back-to-duty therapy was on hold, as I had to now attend therapy for my damn finger. Come on, God, enough was enough.

That Friday, my brother drove me to the fire department clinic to be placed on sick leave from being on POD (injury from performance on duty from my knee). Afterward, he took me to get a rental car. Oh, you know the insurance adjusters were calling my house phone off the ringer. But the lady's insurance handled it as well as my lawyer. Everyone else who was in the car got checked out as well.

As the days went on, the department placed me on the list for the retirement board because of my extended timeframe of being off. You've got to be kidding. How are you going to count POD and SL hours together when it is clear it was not my fault?

My stress level rose as I headed to the retirement board. Yes, they put my name on that list. I did my homework, and I had the CCN police report from the accident with me. Once there, they eased my agitation and anguished by stating that it clearly was not my fault. Therefore, they did not place me on the list for retirement. Hallelujah!

Fortunately, I finished hand therapy and got back to full-duty therapy.

Okay, I had my faith and my guardian angel by my side. Still, there were questions about being a catalyst for punishment. I was in the fire, but where was my voice?

Surgery was next.

CHAPTER 29

My Personal Construction Crew

"But I will not be afraid. God loves and endures forever.
I called in my distress, and he answered and brought me into
a place of safety."

– Psalm 118:4-6

B ack-to-duty physical therapy seemed extremely strenuous for me because my focus was getting clearer so I could have my breast cancer surgery in June. Ortho hand therapy was done. Finally, they cleared me to go back to full-duty fire status. Talk about irons in the fire. Why me?

The fire department clinic knew of my breast cancer diagnosis. The female Physician Assistant who was my attendant at all my appointments was so sympathetic and caring. We continue this friendship to this day. The love and support from family and friends were insurmountable, but it just wasn't enough.

Back at the Fire Prevention office with a façade demeanor; no one had a clue of my misery. It was time. I asked the senior civilian office manager to accompany me to inform the fire marshal. All the inspectors were out in the field, which made it somewhat easier to tell him my news. He had tears, the office manager had tears—we all had tears. He assured me he would take care of everything, including getting the paperwork started for donated leave, which I appreciated. I knew my leave was going to run out, and I could not afford to have leave without pay. The fire marshal instructed me to go home after our discussion to prepare for this new phase in my life. The next day, I was told that the office scheduled a meeting as the battalion chief of the division informed my coworkers of my status. I was told that he even got a little upset while explaining to them. My Fire Prevention family started donating their annual leave. So, with the administrative aspect, everything was in place. I did not have to worry about leave without pay.

God had already foreseen what I was about to foresee!

At my last oncology appointment, I received the preop instructions again: shower the night before surgery and in the morning of surgery with Hibiclens an Antiseptic Skin Cleanser, use a fresh clean towel, and wear another set of fresh clean pajamas. I even had to change my bed linen. For some odd reason, tranquility and peace found me sleeping well. Of course, my prayers were deep and heavy with my rosary underneath my pillow. I was ready for my construction crew.

Morning came so early because of the check-in time at Sibley Hospital. Before leaving home, I repeated the cleansing routine from the night before. My oldest sister picked me up early as the drive to the hospital was a long commute. After arrival, there was a tremendous amount of paperwork to sign and questionnaires to answer. I finally got to sit in the waiting area until it was time. My sister was at the receptionist's desk, having a conversation. The receptionist informed her that my oncologist was the top woman oncologist and the director of Sibley's Sullivan Breast Cancer Center, and women travel from around the world to see her. Wow, that made me feel at ease and comfortable. Trying not to think about the realization of this life-changing surgery, it was time.

My sister went into the back prep room with me. I had already texted my fire prevention close girlfriends, whom I call the FP Divas, to let them know what was transpiring. Even when the nurse administered my IV, I had them on speaker. We laughed, joked, and cut up. My sister even had her share of jokes. You would have thought I was just getting my tonsils out by the way we were acting. Then it was time.

The nurse approached me and said, "Tell them you'll see them later and give the phone to your sister." My sister had already had one of their cell phones numbers, so she could notify the rest of the divas with updates. Sis had to go back into the waiting room. But what still resonates to this day was that the nurse said to me, "I heard you laughing and smiling. With that attitude and positive demeanor, you are going to be all right." I can still picture her saying this to me. Wow!

They did not prepare me for this next step. They wheeled me into another room that had overhead lighting, scopes, and even a breast imaging machine that looked like a mammogram scan. Puzzled and scared, I thought they would do everything while I was under anesthesia. *Nope!* The nurse and physician were outstanding, but that didn't help my anxiety level. The physician had to administer the lumpectomy marker inside my right breast. Again, I had to lay prone and be very still. They said I was going to feel the injection, and they never lied. It felt like the needle (guider) was right near my breast nipple. The pain hit me so hard that all I could do was grimace, accompanied by a loud, moaning monotone. The tears could not even flow. Why me? Why me? Even as I write this, I'm tearing up. Throughout life there will be a lot of experiences you will never forget. This one is forever engrained in my head. The nurse was at my left side, rubbing my back as the moans got louder. Poof, it was done. The guidance marker was in position. Next, they helped me off the table to the imaging machine to make sure it was in the right place. Hell, if it wasn't. The physician stated I was much calmer than expected as he gave me an enormous hug and that's when the tears started flowing.

They wheeled me into the main prep room to meet all the professional medical surgeons—my **construction crew** responsible for putting me back together. My number one artisan, God the Father, has the final diagnosis of my prognosis.

One by one, they came into the prep room to introduce themselves and the scope of work being performed on me. The oncologist, of course, the plastic surgeon, who was top in breast reconstruction and recognized in the Washington Top Doctors, the anesthesiologist, attending nurses, and the radiologist who was the last to come into the room. Being a hazmat technician, the radiologist and I were discussing the isotope being placed in my body during surgery. Because of the minute amount of radiation, I was very familiar with the meters (the dosimeter and Geiger Mueller detector meter) she would use. The topic was the meters as she was going over some of the radiation levels with me. Was this class or surgery? It was time.

The anesthesiologist could not believe the conversation we were exchanging. He said, "Okay, let's break this up, young lady, because I am about to administer the heavy narcotic. Now count to ten backward." No problem. I probably got to eight when it was lights out for me. The mastectomy and lumpectomy went well.

I spent a few days in the hospital. The ride home was driven with caution and care. I tried to listen to my sister's car radio to drown out my negative thoughts, but the mind is so powerful and, if allowed, will take you places near and far. All I could focus on was my appearance, the deformity of my new look. How would this affect my daughters? Can I do this? Will God come back into my life?

As I closed my eyes briefly, my good friend appeared to me. Before his passing, he told me to "Smell the roses now and don't wait until you can't." You've got this, Ruth, because you are God's flower that's ready to blossom. Trying to hold back my tears in the car, a smile appeared. I was going to be all right.

Let me be real here. Cancer tried to win as it knocked on my emotional and physical well-being. My cancer therapy treatment was Tamoxifen. I'm thankful for not receiving chemo or radiation, but I am constantly reminded that a negative environment can change everything. Dancing with glee one minute, the next minute, angry as hell. The muscle and joint aches were indescribable. Sometimes followed by severe cramping in my toes, brought tears my way. I would think about pregnancy when getting calve muscle or toe cramps to point my toes inward and outward. So that's what I did for this affliction. This would make one say bye Felicia to the ecosystem, also known as mother nature. I used to beg for forgiveness for aches when the weather was rainy and cold. Sometimes getting out of bed was a task, but it could be worse. So, I took my time and sat at the end of my bed until my body said *clear*. I felt older than my age, doing any and everything.

When I hear of someone having succumbed to breast cancer, I cringe as it personally affects and scares me. I whisper a soft prayer for them as well as myself.

In this raging fire, I must find my voice.

CHAPTER 30

Ready to Recognize the Reconstruction

The phone calls and visits from family members and friends were an antidote to unconditional love that was well received. The fire marshal's office made sure the leave bank was on point with my donated leave to receive a continuous paycheck. My health insurance was paying its part as well. The meal drop-off was wonderful even though I was somewhat back to cooking. You can't keep this gal down for too long despite feeling wrapped up like a mummy. The bandage was from the upper chest down, surpassing the belly button. So far, my adversities have been panning out. My daughters had a significant role in my healing despite the façade I hide well.

My body had to heal before going for the second surgery: September 2015. Again, my oldest sibling drove me back to Sibley and waited for me because it was in/out. This time, my mind was ready.

I had my discharge instructions and scheduled appointments with the plastic surgeon. Another bandage, but with an added device—a draining tube under my skin attached to a drainage bulb that hung outside the bandages. The Jackson-Pratt Drain. This is the routine procedure that prepares one for breast expanders or new boobies. Finally arriving home, my sister asked if she needed to stay a while. Nope. I even locked the door as she left and lay on the couch to wait for my daughters to come home. Boy, did I kid myself? The dizziness and nauseous feeling became overbearing. Glad the phone was next to my sofa. I was calling my girlfriends that lived nearby to help me. Finally, I reached my girlfriend, and her daughter, who lived in my neighborhood, came to my desperate rescue. It was a struggle to open the front door, as my knees felt like buckling. They assisted me upstairs to my bedroom to rest. My girlfriend helped me put on my pajamas while her daughter bought up some soup and crackers. My sister wanted to know why I did not call her back to return. I misjudged myself big time. Put that pride aside and let them help you. My girlfriend was willing to stay overnight, but one of my daughters finally arrived home. Later that evening, I was feeling much better as the other two daughters came home.

My instructions were to call the office if I had a fever higher than 101 degrees Fahrenheit, if there was a cloudy, foul odor from the drainage tube or the bulb, or if the drainage tube became dislodged or fell off. Otherwise, the drainage bulb had to be looked at, measured, recorded, and emptied two to three times per day. Morning, before bed, and sometimes in between, if the bulb was full to the top with drainage. Guess who did this procedure? Me. I refused to allow my daughters to help. Besides, I did not feel like reviving either of them if they fainted at the sight of the blood and fluid drainage. Hell, they call me to kill a spider. So, after checking my temperature, then with the measuring cup and the Jackson-Pratt drain record sheet, the job had to be done.

Inside my bathroom, with a closed door and sanitized area, I unattached the bulb carefully to visually measure the amount of drainage inside the measuring container. Then I recorded the volume level of drainage and poured the contents into the toilet. This was repetitious and necessary because it had to be turned in at each visit. I was glad the viscosity was thinning, and the bleeding was ceasing until nothing remained, which was a good sign of healing. But the mental and emotional toll it took on me, especially at night; I literally would cry myself to sleep. I felt so alone, yet I wasn't as my daughters were in the other room. Family and friends never left my side, yet I felt isolated. Crying out constantly, "Why me?" every night became my personal anthem. The bitterness and anger between me and my faith was unreal. I really had it in for God to allow this to happen to me. Was praying a waste of time? There were no sentiments at all. Why did you fail me? What did I do to deserve this? My emotional and mental state was declining. It was bad. My hugs came from me. The pep talks came from me. There was no choice in the matter. I had to rediscover my voice for self-love. That fierce, flawless woman firefighter had to make a comeback. Eventually, I did, but it was a really slow process.

The plastic surgeon visits consisted of injecting the liquid solution to slowly help enhance the expander. I was told to take a Percocet an hour before arriving. Okay, but my pain threshold had a high tolerance, but I obeyed the instructions, and, boy, glad I listened. I hardly felt the injection of the solution into the expander until on the ride home. I remember talking with my sister, and then the uneasy feeling hit me. *Come on Perc, please work*, I kept thinking. This indefinable pain hit me to the point where my conversation halted. I told her what was going on as the continued ride home was in silence from me. Feeling your skin stretch was like feeling birth contractions and dilation. This happened until the expander (can't remember how many months it took) had met the desired breast size. My sister and my brother took turns being my chauffeur as Percocet became my friend. Finally, that day came, which was filled with anxiety and fear. Removing the bandages. The thought of being disfigured was overwhelming. Here it goes!

The nurse called me back to the exam room to remove the bandages and tube. With my head turned and fighting back tears, she said, "Take your time, but look at yourself in the floor-length mirror in the exam room." She had finished removing everything. Removing the connected tube inside my body didn't hurt at all. The pain was trying to build up my confidence to look at the new me in the mirror. I am a warrior, I am strong, I used to run in burning raging fires, I had babies, don't lose control. With closed, tearful eyes, I looked in the mirror and saw *myself*. My smile overpowered my disillusionment. I looked good. Bellowing out, "Where are my scars and the huge deformity?"

The nurse smiled at me, kissed me on my cheek, and said, "I told you. You are beautiful."

Then my plastic surgeon came into the room. Each time (even to this day) she takes photos at all angles of my breast for my portfolio and medical reasons. You can't tell the reconstruction unless I mention it. My scars had healed with very few keloids. I didn't need a breast nipple tattoo. She said, "You don't listen because I told you I was going to try my damnedest to preserve," and she did.

Even though I chose reconstruction, the battle scars have been accepted as my reminder of my intense battle. While I give out mad love for the other breast cancer warriors that chose no reconstruction as their reminder.

Throughout my ordeal, especially on restless nights, my cell phone became my close friend. I would read up on breast cancer liturgy and research. One night, an article showed up on my cell about a woman firefighter (from another state) who was diagnosed with breast cancer and experiencing serious issues within her department. Thereafter, other articles were coming in. Wow, I am not alone with this disease coming from a fire career.

Breast cancer is finally being recognized as one of the toxic carcinogens, along with lung and prostate cancer. So, my crying out, "Why me?" transitioned to "Why not me?" Become that vessel for others and help them release their personal health bondage. That's when I did a serious self-gentrification—refining myself, being positive, increasing self-wealth, reflecting, respecting, and renovating myself. This is where I understood the assignment that God was placing on me. He said, "You have this voice, so use it."

Talk about an epiphany!

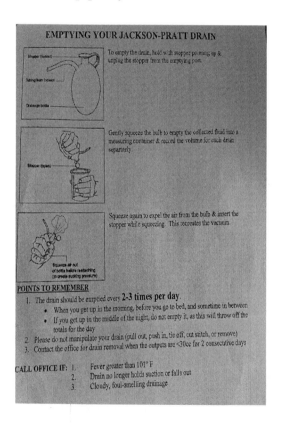

EMPTYING YOUR JACKSON-PRATT DRAIN

To empty the drain, hold with stopper pointing up & unplug the stopper from the emptying port.

Gently squeeze the bulb to empty the collected fluid into a measuring container & record the volume for each drain separately.

Squeeze again to expel the air from the bulb & insert the stopper while squeezing. This recreates the vacuum.

POINTS TO REMEMBER
1. The drain should be emptied every **2-3 times per day**.
   - When you get up in the morning, before you go to bed, and sometime in between
   - If you get up in the middle of the night, do not empty it, as this will throw off the totals for the day
2. Please do not manipulate your drain (pull out, push in, tie off, cut stitch, or remove)
3. Contact the office for drain removal when the outputs are <30cc for 2 consecutive days

CALL OFFICE IF:
1. Fever greater than 101° F
2. Drain no longer holds suction or falls out
3. Cloudy, foul-smelling drainage

JACKSON PRATT DRAIN RECORD

DATE	Drain #1	Drain #2	Drain #3	Drain #4
	AM ___ cc Midday ___ cc PM ___ cc	AM ___ cc Midday ___ cc PM ___ cc	AM ___ cc Midday ___ cc PM ___ cc	AM ___ cc Midday ___ cc PM ___ cc
	AM ___ cc Midday ___ cc PM ___ cc	AM ___ cc Midday ___ cc PM ___ cc	AM ___ cc Midday ___ cc PM ___ cc	AM ___ cc Midday ___ cc PM ___ cc
	AM ___ cc Midday ___ cc PM ___ cc	AM ___ cc Midday ___ cc PM ___ cc	AM ___ cc Midday ___ cc PM ___ cc	AM ___ cc Midday ___ cc PM ___ cc
	AM ___ cc Midday ___ cc PM ___ cc	AM ___ cc Midday ___ cc PM ___ cc	AM ___ cc Midday ___ cc PM ___ cc	AM ___ cc Midday ___ cc PM ___ cc
	AM ___ cc Midday ___ cc PM ___ cc	AM ___ cc Midday ___ cc PM ___ cc	AM ___ cc Midday ___ cc PM ___ cc	AM ___ cc Midday ___ cc PM ___ cc
	AM ___ cc Midday ___ cc PM ___ cc	AM ___ cc Midday ___ cc PM ___ cc	AM ___ cc Midday ___ cc PM ___ cc	AM ___ cc Midday ___ cc PM ___ cc
	AM ___ cc Midday ___ cc PM ___ cc	AM ___ cc Midday ___ cc PM ___ cc	AM ___ cc Midday ___ cc PM ___ cc	AM ___ cc Midday ___ cc PM ___ cc
	AM ___ cc Midday ___ cc PM ___ cc	AM ___ cc Midday ___ cc PM ___ cc	AM ___ cc Midday ___ cc PM ___ cc	AM ___ cc Midday ___ cc PM ___ cc
	AM ___ cc Midday ___ cc PM ___ cc	AM ___ cc Midday ___ cc PM ___ cc	AM ___ cc Midday ___ cc PM ___ cc	AM ___ cc Midday ___ cc PM ___ cc
	AM ___ cc Midday ___ cc PM ___ cc	AM ___ cc Midday ___ cc PM ___ cc	AM ___ cc Midday ___ cc PM ___ cc	AM ___ cc Midday ___ cc PM ___ cc
	AM ___ cc Midday ___ cc PM ___ cc	AM ___ cc Midday ___ cc PM ___ cc	AM ___ cc Midday ___ cc PM ___ cc	AM ___ cc Midday ___ cc PM ___ cc
	AM ___ cc Midday ___ cc PM ___ cc	AM ___ cc Midday ___ cc PM ___ cc	AM ___ cc Midday ___ cc PM ___ cc	AM ___ cc Midday ___ cc PM ___ cc
	AM ___ cc Midday ___ cc PM ___ cc	AM ___ cc Midday ___ cc PM ___ cc	AM ___ cc Midday ___ cc PM ___ cc	AM ___ cc Midday ___ cc PM ___ cc
	AM ___ cc Midday ___ cc PM ___ cc	AM ___ cc Midday ___ cc PM ___ cc	AM ___ cc Midday ___ cc PM ___ cc	AM ___ cc Midday ___ cc PM ___ cc
	AM ___ cc Midday ___ cc PM ___ cc	AM ___ cc Midday ___ cc PM ___ cc	AM ___ cc Midday ___ cc PM ___ cc	AM ___ cc Midday ___ cc PM ___ cc

BRING THIS SHEET WITH YOU TO YOUR APPOINTMENT

137

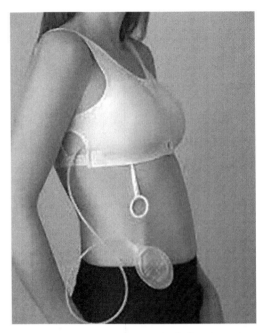

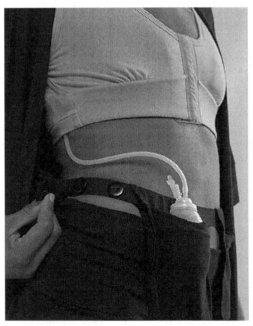

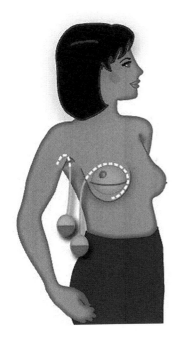

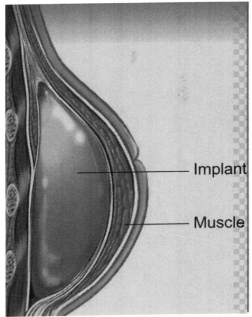

Implant

Muscle

CHAPTER 31

Channeling My Inner Essence With Gratitude, Robustness, and Poise

"No temptation has come upon you except what is common to men. But God is faithful, and he not let you be tempted beyond what you can bear, but along with the temptation, God will make the way out so that you may be able to endure it."

— 1 Corinthians 13

M y road to destiny was rocky, full of ups and downs, and speed bumps along the way, but with patience, time, acceptance, and renewed faith, the road gracefully smoothed out. Personal perception and healing will allow you to gravitate toward a full acceptance of the new you in dealing with any health issues. The year 2015 defined this for me. I finally allowed my heart and demeanor of my struggles to change the trajectory of my old lifestyle to live and love life one day at a time. Learning to quit focusing on being angry with God and myself, I learned to navigate my direction and purpose instead of drowning in sorrow or shame. It taught me bravery, transparency, elevation, and aspiration. Recognize that you are never alone. I'll admit that there are days of slipping back, which is a normal human reaction, but the goal is to regain dominance to move forward. I constantly must repeat and promote this positivity on my visual vision board so that my reward is at the end of my rainbow, and I can smile, shine, and radiate again.

The year 2016 allowed me to be:

BOLD:

Becoming Overflowed with Life's Dreams—for me. I can see purpose and clarity again. I wear my clothes with pride instead of shame because of my surgeries and my body's appearance. My family is doing great and succeeding. My surgical scars have healed on a medical aspect, with set oncology appointments every six months and plastic surgeon appointments once a year. God has forgiven me as I have forgiven myself. That year was monumental, as I officially retired—twenty-seven years at the Fire Department (not one ounce of disability).

Since retirement, I have had the honor and privilege of being a guest speaker at Breast Cancer events and podcasts.

S.I.S.= She is Strength!

My goal is to continue being an advocate for Breast Cancer Awareness for individuals of all races, ethnicities, and ages, and for women firefighters. My story shows my imperfections to perfection and the belief that life is out here waiting for me and you.

AFFIRMATIONS

Always put God first and not idolize man or material things.

Start journaling as it becomes your initial road to healing and telling your story.

2011: I began journaling my life

2015: My journal became a dream

2016: My journal became a goal

2022: My journal is becoming a reality

Do not allow others to rush your process of healing. Be strong when you are ready: remember you are not healing for them but for you, so do not become complacent.

Release those convoluted ideas of yourself.

Try to remain true to your game and manifest the outlook and outcome.

Claim abundance.

Continue to dance.

Go from crying tears to drying tears that will perpetuate your beautiful view and existence.

Inhale your inner beauty that God has placed on you, above you, and for you. Remember, everyone has some sort of imperfection.

Start becoming your personal advocate, being the frontliner of your health, mind, body, and soul.

Learn to accept some setbacks as it's a steppingstone and catalyst for success.

DDs: D̲on't let your D̲iagnosis D̲efine Your D̲ignity/ D̲ecorum.

Guard your energy from negative acrimonious vibes.

Create your personal vision board and claim it. How I executed this by starting with the first letter of my name— write down positive, pragmatic, energetic words ex, Ruth: I am resplendent, robust, reformed, resourceful, respectable, resilient, and revolutionized because I Am Ruth!

Let go and Let God.

Find your prism of rainbow, meaning your circle of faithful family and friends.

WITHIN THE FLAMES, I FOUND MY VOICE
As my journey continues.

About the Author

Ruth Redmond, a native of Washington, DC, grew up in Southeast. She is a mother of three lovely daughters and a fun-loving, energetic grandmother. A twenty-seven-year career from the DCFD & EMS Department, starting out as a career women firefighter; female fire investigator, hazardous material technician and retired as an International Code Council and Charter School fire inspector. Being a true Libran, Ruth thrives on balance in all aspects; a caring, doting friend, sister, aunt, and godmother; avid music lover of all genres from classical to go-go; graceful and classy with a sense of humor despite her pitfalls.

Ruth's belief in survivorship after being diagnosed with breast cancer has given her the honor of being guest speakers on numerous platforms.

She wrote this memoir of aspiration to inspiration so others know it is okay to set boundaries and fully believe in themselves, and to utilize their personal mantra in the promotion of health, wealth, faith, and physical and mental stabilities. "Become your advocate of your path—live through your journey to fine your voice."

Made in the USA
Middletown, DE
05 November 2023

41759362R00092